The Essential Principles of Graphic Design

Debbie Millman

Logo concept: Ea Feua

BOOKS

Cincinnati, Ohio

www.howdesign.com

For more fine books from F+W Publications, visit www.fwbookstore.com.

12 11 10 09 08   5 4 3 2 1

Distributed in Canada by Fraser Direct
100 Armstrong Avenue
Georgetown, Ontario, Canada L7G 5S4
Tel: (905) 877-4411

Distributed in Australia by Capricorn Link
P.O. Box 704, Windsor, NSW 2756 Australia
Tel: (02) 4577-3555

ISBN-10: 1-60061-047-1
ISBN-13: 978-1-60061-047-9

This book was set in Chronicle typeface, designed by Hoefler & Frere Jones

Edited by Jonathan Ingoldby
Designed by Rodrigo Corral Design

Production coordinated by RotoVision SA

F+W PUBLICATIONS, INC.

Contents

First Person

When I was 12 years old, I had a best friend named Debbie. We both adored magazines and fashion, and we loved to paint, read, and write. We spent the summer before we entered sixth grade creating a magazine, which, primarily because of our names, we titled *Debutante*. Many painstaking hours were devoted to writing articles in longhand and doing illustrations. We interviewed everyone we knew for "tell all" exposés, and initiated surveys about clothes, boys, and dating (though neither of us had yet tested those romantic waters). We scoured magazines and books for ideas, dreamily obsessed with our invention. We enjoyed making decisions about what to include and what to leave out, what was culturally important and what wasn't, and the only fight we ever had involved who was going to retain ownership of the sole original copy. As the summer ended, my love affair with the printed word took hold.

By the time I got to college, I was determined to become a modern-day version of Diana Vreeland, the legendary *Vogue* editor. I eagerly made my way to the offices of the university newspaper, but I was kindly and very politely rebuked. I was so desperate to work for the paper that I imagined writing gloriously heady letters to the editor that would so enthrall the staff they would beg me to join them. My ambitious longing finally paid off when no one on the paper wanted to cover a women's rights rally, and I was called at the last minute to report on the feminist political uprising outside the campus health-food store.

Upon graduation, I dropped off my portfolio at Condé Nast, as was their company policy. Miraculously, I got a call to come in for an interview with human resources; apparently, Charles Churchward, the design director at *Vanity Fair*, saw something in my book he liked. This, to me, was the equivalent of winning the lottery. I spent every waking hour prior to the interview agonizing over the contents of my "career wardrobe," posing in outfit after outfit in an effort to ensure I would make the best possible impression. These outfits consisted of the clothes my mother lovingly handmade as a graduation gift, and the morning of the interview I chose the royal blue bolero jacket; matching A-line knee-length skirt; a beige faux-silk blouse with blue pin dots and a big, floppy bow on the front; sheer black stockings; and flat black patent-leather loafers. I anxiously gazed at myself in the mirror before leaving my mother's Queens apartment and took a deep breath. I knew that what happened next could change my life forever. As I sat on the cramped, balmy Express Bus into Manhattan, I fantasized about befriending the human resources director; being invited up to meet Mr. Churchward; getting hired as his crackerjack assistant; working late nights and weekends; cavorting with the glamorous editors, art directors, and designers; and, of course, spending my entire career being fabulously successful at the best magazine company in the whole wide world.

I exited the bus on 42nd Street and Madison Avenue and skipped toward the Condé Nast building, faux-silk bow billowing in the July breeze and a faux-leather portfolio banging against my legs, when the unthinkable happened. I tripped. I toppled so hard and so fast that three passers-by came to help me. As they asked me if I was OK, I felt my stinging knee and burning face and knew without looking: I had an ugly bruise on my leg and a vicious tear up my stockings. I didn't have time to change my hose, but quickly realized that both my skirt and the tactical placement of my portfolio could mask the bruise. I lumbered on and made it to my appointment on time. When I met the human resources director, I was mesmerized. She was unlike any other woman I had ever encountered. She was breezy and elegant and alluring in her pale yellow sleeveless shift. She had the thinnest arms I had ever seen and the biggest office I had ever been in. She invited me to sit down and I complied; and as I tumbled back into the orange overstuffed sofa I felt the hole in my stockings widen and prayed that she didn't hear the ripping sound. She quickly looked through my portfolio without uttering a syllable, and when she was finished she shut it with a thud. She looked me up and down, and we had the following conversation:

She: "So. What kind of design do you want to do?"

Me: "Excuse me?"

She: "What kind of design do you want to do?"

Me: "Kind of design?"

She [with a furrowed brow]: "Yes."

Me: "Hmm. Um. I think I would like to do any kind of design."

She [with a very furrowed brow]: "You can't do any kind of design. You have to pick."

Me: "Pick?"

She [clearly annoyed]: "Yes. You have to pick. You have to pick editorial design, or promotional design, or advertising, or custom publishing. You must choose one."

Me [thinking to myself]: Well I really want to say "editorial" but maybe I'm not good enough and though I don't know what custom publishing or promotional design are I will say "promotional" but really I would happily sweep the floors if they want me to.

Me [actually speaking]: "Um. Promotional?"

And then I couldn't help myself. I continued talking.

Me: "But I would do anything. Anything you need."

And then there was silence.

She: "Well. Yes, then. I see."

And with that, she sighed and made one sweeping gesture for me to take my portfolio back. I looked at her and picked it up. Though she said she would be in touch, I knew at that moment that I was not going to hear from her, and I never did. I made some small talk as I was escorted out; I remember asking her how long she had been at Condé Nast and I remember her replying "Twelve years," with a clip in her voice.

Several months later, in a moment of aberrant fearlessness, I got up my nerve and called her, but the person who answered the phone told me she no longer worked there. By then I had gotten my first job as a traffic girl at a fledgling cable magazine and worked late nights and weekends, and cavorted with the editors, art directors, and designers; and, of course, I didn't spend the rest of my career there. But when I worked there, I joyfully learned about editorial design, and promotional design, and advertising, and even custom publishing. I realized how much I did know and how much I didn't know, and embarked upon what has become a lifelong journey in learning about the abundant and bewitching specialties in the marvelous discipline that is considered graphic design.

Twenty-five years after that decisive day, I've come to the realization that my ill-fated interview did indeed impact the rest of my life, just not in the way I intended. But this is the most interesting thing about possibilities: there is always something new to dream of.

Consider this book a primer on the variety of opportunities available to designers working today. As you peruse these pages and ponder the diverse directions for a career in graphic design, try to experiment with your many options. But please consider this: you never, ever have to pick just one.

ESSENTIAL PRINCIPLES

Introduction

The practice of graphic design is both a science and an art. The ability to convey ideas through images requires designers to be simultaneously creative and logical as they weave visual and intellectual messages.

The individual building blocks of graphic design are also multidimensional. Color, typography, layout, and style demand a thorough education in and of themselves, and then an understanding of the comprehensive way in which they must seamlessly and organically work together.

To the untrained eye, choices about the various elements that make up a design often seem rather mysterious; in fact, those unaware of the formalities of design might consider that the primary skill of the designer is to make something look "right." And while that may be the case, the skill in achieving this observable balance is hardly perceptive.

Nor is it prescriptive. While there are acknowledged best practices for achieving excellence, there are few "one size fits all" methodologies guaranteeing design greatness. In fact, two of the essential principles of graphic design cannot be taught: passion and empathy. And yet both are critical components of achieving design distinction. Design without passion is simply manipulative persuasion. Design without empathy leaves the designer without the ability to telegraphically connect one mind with another. At the same time, the skills that can be taught, such as working within the luminous world of pigments, or managing the intellectual, physical, and stylistic aesthetics of form, language, and image, are robustly complex and can take a lifetime to master. However, the more information we have, and the more access to information we have, the more capacity we will have to create a meaningful representation of the world through design.

Graphic design has the unique ability to reflect the culture in which we participate. This evokes an unparalleled composition of sensory perceptions. Color, typography, layout, and style all contribute to the modern expression of design, and our society. The extension of any one of these sensory perceptions vastly impacts the way we think and act—and the way we perceive the world around us. When these perceptions change, people change; consequently, the world changes. The following pages contain a fundamental overview of the basic components of graphic communication. Like design, the utilization of each element is a science and an art—and a craft. Each must be mastered, and all are infinite in their application.

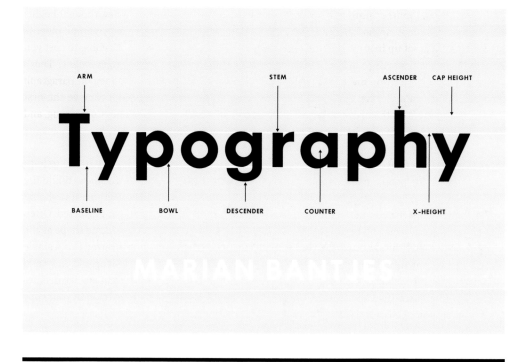

Typography is like writing. You learn the basics to construct some simple sentences; you learn more to be a little more eloquent; you practice, following a dizzying formula of rules and exceptions to rules; and eventually you learn to break the rules and leap off into personal expression. There is, unfortunately, not enough space in these few pages to teach you even the basics of typography, so I have chosen instead to write an impassioned plea to keep you from harming me—and others— with some common bad practices. Poor typography makes me wince with pain.

The first thing I need to do is to tell you to forget everything your high-school typing teacher ever taught you. The typewriter, while all very well for secretaries in the 1970s, is a primitive machine. Think of it as a bumper car. You're grown up now, and you're in the driving seat of a Ferrari. Learn to drive it without bumping into things.

There are many things to unlearn. To start, do not put two spaces after periods. Stop it right now and please don't let me ever see it again. Next, unless you are being "avant garde," do not underline text for emphasis or for book or magazine titles. Use italics. Always use italics for the titles, sometimes use bold for emphasis, though italics are usually better. And do not use a tab for paragraph indents; tabs have specific purposes and indenting paragraphs is not one of them. Do not argue with me on this. Do as you're told.

There is a reason for determining the beginning of a paragraph: to indicate "a new thought begins here." So do use some method, but let's pretend for a moment that line spaces, paragraph indents (which should be set up in style sheets), and dingbats cost money. Say $100. It's going to cost you $100 each time you start a paragraph. Would you use a line space and a paragraph indent? That's $200! Don't do it. Use one method, it's all you need. Another way to save money on paragraph indents is that when you have a section start, or a heading, you can (should) remove the first paragraph indent after the break or heading. Don't look at *The New Yorker*. They do it wrong, and they are personally responsible for raising my blood pressure.

Make sure you use true quotation marks and apostrophes. This is so basic it saddens me to have to explain it. Some people call them "smart quotes," but the moniker is unnecessary. While the specific appearance of quotation marks varies between typefaces, the closing mark(s) should match the shape of the comma, and the opening mark(s) should be the same but inverted. Often they look like little sixes and nines, but not always. An apostrophe is always the same shape as the comma, and exactly the same as a single closing quotation mark (when it is inverted it is a single opening quote, not an apostrophe). Those other things, which usually go straight up and down and do not have the same shape as the comma, are called primes or double primes, and are like needles in my eyes when used instead of quotation marks and apostrophes. When I see them in your copy I feel physical pain. I am not kidding. Please.

There is a correct use for primes: to denote inches and feet, as well as seconds (both as a measure of time and a subunit of degrees): for instance, I am 5′ 4″ tall (prime = feet, double prime = inches). The subtorture of this genre is to see inches or feet represented by quotation marks and apostrophes. I am not 5' 4" tall—that is completely senseless. The point is, the marks are not style; they have meaning. Speaking of which, the meaning of quotation marks is to indicate that something was said (or thought, or quoted as an example), not, as so many people seem to believe, to add emphasis. See above: italics (or bold) for emphasis; quotation marks to quote something. They are also useful to indicate sarcasm—which is usually the unintended effect when mistakenly using them for emphasis. "Fresh" fish is "so-called fresh" fish; i.e. it is anything but fresh. I see this in stores every day and it would be laughable if it didn't hurt so much.

Many people are confused about the use of dashes, but really it's very simple. Hyphens (-) are used to keep things together, em-dashes (—) are used to keep things apart, and en-dashes (–) are used to indicate a range. If you can replace the dash with the word "to," it should be an en-dash (most common in number ranges: "1963–2007"). If the dash creates a pause or an aside, it should be an em-dash. But if you're making one thing out of two, it should be a hyphen. So simple. The double hyphen, used in typing, should be changed to an em-dash. Some people—and I am not one of them—prefer to use an en-dash with space on either side in place of an em-dash. To this I say, "Don't be such a wimp, use the proper character." [Editor's note: in many English-speaking countries, an en-dash with space on either side is the accepted form of punctuation for indicating a pause or aside.]

When it comes to setting body copy, do not make us all dizzy and sick with variable spacing between letters from line to line. Please change the default Justification settings in your page layout program to have letter spacing be zero percent across the board. That is, the spacing between your letters should neither squeeze nor wander, no matter what you see in newspapers and the *Auto Trader*. Type designers spend a lot of time figuring out the correct fit from letter to letter; please respect their expertise (and if you've ever heard type designer Lucas de Groot speak on the subject of kerning pairs you will join me in groveling into the corner where we belong).

However, remember that using shorter line lengths can cause problems with word spacing. Getting gappy lines in your justified text? Increase your line length, reduce your type size, add some hyphenation, and when in doubt, set the text ragged.

Did I hear you gasp when I said the word "hyphenation"? Do not get me started on the ridiculous vendetta against hyphens in the corporate world. Get thee to a book, a decent magazine or newspaper. Check it out: hyphens! An army of glorious little hyphens are there every day, helping to protect us from the evils of word spacing. We hardly notice them, we're so used to their service for us. If you're using justified text, turn the hyphenation on, allow no more than two or three in a row, and you have done us all a great service. But if you're working under a hyphen ban, just set the text ragged and spare us from falling into the pools of white space between your words.

Ragged text can (preferably would) be hyphenated too, especially in shorter line lengths, but what simply amazes me is how often I'm assaulted by small blocks of display text that are unnecessarily hyphenated, badly hyphenated, or with poor line breaks without regard to how the text looks or reads. Extended text is one thing, give it the attention you can, but if a small block of text stands alone as display, or even a caption, check each and every line, taking into account how it reads, what information belongs together, and what the final shape of the thing is. Shape? Yes, shape! What should the shape of a small piece of display type be? Generally speaking, short and fat. It should have shorter lines at top and bottom, and bulge out a little in the middle. We're thinking middle-aged man here, not curvy woman, not exploding sled, not phallus. Short and fat.

There is a fashion for excessive leading in body text which shocks me to the core. Stripes. Stripes! Why would you want to read long bodies of horizontal stripes? The entire point of setting body text is to aid the reader. The text block should be cohesive, with just enough room to breathe between lines, but not so much as to make our eyes hop from one line to the next. That is just so tiring.

Lists and bullets and hangs. Let's think about bullets and hangs: first thing, they go together, joined in their mutual violence. Don't use bullets without hanging the following text, and make sure the hang aligns correctly under the first line. Same with numbered lists, and be particularly aware if your numbers are going to go into double or triple digits. Figure it out in advance, then set a tab so your numbers align right to the last digit or period or whatever mark follows it, then give yourself about an en- to an em-space and set another tab for your text to align left on. Lock it and load it. Speaking of which, bullets are bullets, not cannonballs, so keep them small! Big enough that you can see them, but not so big they scare the living daylights out of someone. The point is to create hierarchy and order, so keep it neat and tidy.

If at all possible, do not bludgeon me with ALL CAPS if you have true small capitals at hand. They come as a separate font in Type 1 format, or are included in most Open Type fonts. If you don't have them, don't fake them by making shrunken capitals or by using that stupid button in QuarkXPress. In that case, all caps will do. But whichever you choose, give them a little letter spacing: 50 to 100 units if used within body text, perhaps more if used as a heading.

Whatever you do, keep it consistent. Consistency is the key to everything. Don't use all caps here and small caps there. If you use old style figures (numbers), use them throughout (and generally, if you're using old style figures you should also be using small caps; all caps and old style figures look terrible together). If you use italics for emphasis, use them throughout. Make a decision and stick to it; or, if you change your style, change it throughout.

Now, a word or two on display text—that is, text which stands alone from body copy, usually at larger sizes than the text. Where earlier I asked you to trust the letter spacing of the type designer, at larger sizes most type needs some adjustment. The first thing it needs is overall letter tightening; the bigger it is, the more you need to track it in. Then, it almost always needs some manual kerning. Look at the type, fuss with it, add space between letters that touch or come too close to each other, tighten it where they wander away. Similarly, you probably need to tighten the leading in larger type, and again, the bigger the size, the smaller the ratio between size and leading. Fuss, fuss, fuss. Display text is on display! Don't embarrass the type by leaving it unattended, standing out on its own like a girl with her dress tucked into the back of her underwear.

There is so much more to know, but these basic things will alleviate a lot of pain. For more, you should read *The Elements of Typographic Style* by Robert Bringhurst (read all of it, and keep a copy at hand), *Thinking with Type* by Ellen Lupton, and of course everything else you can get your hands on in regards to typography. You stand, with typographers everywhere, to keep the barbarians from the gates. Spare us all from the invasion of typographic atrocities.

Go. Do good, and do well.

LISA ROUSSEAU

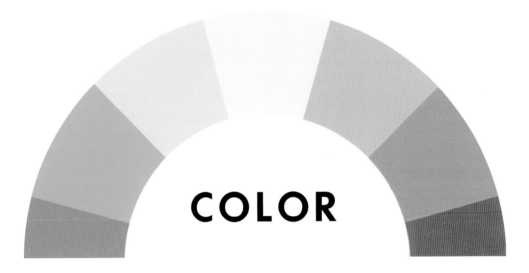

COLOR

I knew very early on in my life that art, in some way, shape, or form, was my calling. I went about it in an unusual way though, starting in print reproduction as a press-man (woman). I loved the idea of transferring big blobs of ink through a tube into a machine and having the ability to manage the transference of that ink onto paper to reproduce anything. I worked in partnership with the originator to achieve their aesthetic goals.

Color variables are infinite. From looking at the world and identifying with colors, to specifying a color and breaking down its properties so that it can be printed is, for me, a complete process. In some weird way I felt like the artist in the equation.

Personal connections and cultural backgrounds influence how we interpret colors. Color affects everything. Depending on where we live in the world, we bring our perceptions and bias toward color into every situation. Colors have diverse meanings in many cultures and in different parts of the world. Perceptions of color are subjective; therefore there are some colors that have universal appeal and others that do not. We in the western world may deem a color appropriate, but that color may have a significant negative impact in another part of the world. Color selection has to connect with your audience. When working for a client or doing self-promotion, make sure you get input upfront about retaining a "known" color, or coming up with a new color expression. Determine what role color plays in the design's environment, and find out what that color signifies in the rest of the world. Be responsible, do your homework, and get feedback.

Color is everywhere. What would our life and our world be without it? How would we reference things? Color is the reflection of light. Rainbows are created when white light is split up by droplets of water. When all colors are present in the visible light spectrum, it is perceived as white. In the graphic design industry, white is considered to be the absence of color and a would-be surface to apply colors to until otherwise specified.

The significance of individual colors in western societies has changed over the years, but the following are generally accurate.

BLACK is the color of authority and power. It is popular in fashion because it makes people appear thinner. Black is timeless. Priests wear black to signify submission to God.

WHITE is worn by Western brides to symbolize innocence and purity. White reflects light and is considered a summer color. Doctors and nurses wear white to imply sterility.

RED is the color of love. Red cars are popular targets for thieves and supposedly get pulled over more often by police who assume they are speeding.

PINK is a romantic color. It symbolizes appreciation, thanks, grace, happiness, admiration, love, friendship, harmony, and compassion.

BLUE is one of the most popular colors. It causes the opposite reaction to red. Peaceful, tranquil blue causes the body to produce calming chemicals. Blue is the color of the sky and the ocean.

GREEN symbolizes nature. It is a calming, refreshing color. People waiting to appear on TV sit in "green rooms" to relax. Hospitals often use green because it relaxes patients.

YELLOW is an attention-getter and is considered an optimistic color. It is the most difficult color for the eye to take in, so it can be overpowering if overused.

PURPLE is the color of royalty. It connotes luxury, wealth, and sophistication. It is considered feminine and romantic.

BROWN is the color of earth and is abundant in nature. Brown symbolizes home and friendship. Light brown implies genuineness, while dark brown is similar to wood or leather and has the same reassuring solidity. Amber, a golden brown, represents courage and energy.

Colors can also be said to have certain aspects, such as "warm" or "cool." Warm colors reside in the red area of the color spectrum, and include orange and yellow. Cool colors inhabit the blue area of the spectrum and include purple and green. Colors such as gray and brown are considered "neutral."

A major factor in printing color is the paper itself. White paper acts as the "white" of your image, which is why bright white papers yield the best results. Glossy white papers allow ink to sit on top of the paper, which makes the colors appear more vibrant. Matte paper often provides better quality for handling a document, and the ink dries faster, but such paper has a high absorption level that embeds the ink into the paper, acting rather like a sponge. This can have a dulling effect on colors, and make the edges of an image look less crisp. It really is amazing how far an image can stray from the intended appearance if the wrong paper is used. Therefore, sourcing the right paper is an essential element of design in relation to color that should not be overlooked. Consult your printer first for guidance.

Creation and implementation go hand in hand, as far as I'm concerned. One does not limit the other. I could go on and on about color, and printing. When I was a press-woman, I would look at the work and study the decisions that must have been made to create what I was printing. After a while, I couldn't take it. I had to design! As crazy as I thought my path was, it really did became a holistic/cathartic approach to design. I just happened to start at the end and work my way back to the beginning. The deconstruction of the "end," for me, strengthened the beginning. If a design cannot be printed, it remains stagnant. Print liberates the idea of the design. That is how meaningful messages are conveyed.

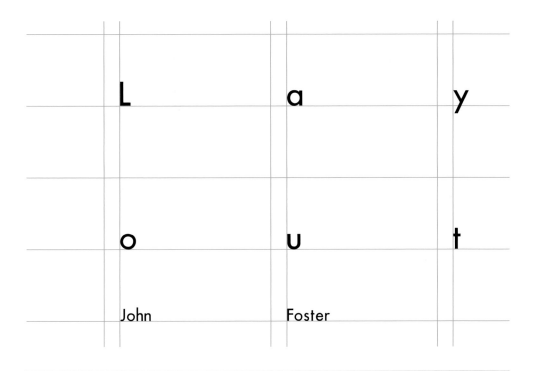

Your hands are hovering next to one another. What had seemed like an innocent lunch now seems like so much more. If you were to pick up that knife sitting beside your pristine plate you could cut through the sexual tension and serve it up as an appetizer. You reach across the invisible boundary that has defined your relationship up until this point and you touch. It is just a matter of inches reaching gently through the air, yet nothing will ever be the same. It means something, this subtle move. It means everything.

We live our lives governed by simple rules that determine the repercussions of our every move. Spending the bulk of our days abiding by these rules is, in essence, what makes the world go round. It is the way people get along and work together and function in social and business settings. However, it is the few occasions when we do not play by the rules, like the bad little boys and girls we long to be, that truly define our lives.

If you haven't yet caught on to how this relates to layout, then you know so little about design (and about life) that it is painful.

As a society, we barely notice when things are "right." This is how things are supposed to be. In layout, we don't notice when elements are lined up and locked in a synchronized dance, somehow frozen in perfect harmony. Yet the slightest movement of one piece of type or the slight rotation of a graphic element creates a world of possibilities. Is it tension?

Joyhopesorrowviolencepassion??? One thing is for certain. It is something! You know how you know? Because you just feel it. It is a simple, yet amazingly effective, tool. Like any tool, it has to be used in the proper hands to truly harness the power available.

Picasso went through the arduous process of learning to paint in a realistic manner before he felt comfortable expanding the human form in ways that forever changed the manner in which we view the figure. You, the day-to-day designer, should take note and study the masters of the basic tenets of layout. Meet the Swiss.

Certainly, some form of layout—the organization of objects on a flat form—existed on runic tablets, Egyptian scrolls, and those insanely detailed hand-drawn pages of the Bible (gratuitous gold foil, anyone?). However, in modern times, it was the Swiss that bared the white space naked before us and then began to structure elements upon it (Helvetica, anyone?) in such an organized fashion that the foundation of page design was finally revealed to us. One of the designers in my office has a poster filled with tiny thumbnails of classic Swiss designs from the past, and I never cease to be amazed how these designs, that were intended to be viewed as posters 4ft (1.2m) tall, work just as well as postage stamps. So tight is the adherence to simple grid lines, so perfect the balance between so few items, that they simply cannot fail. Take the squint test, assuming sitting in front of a computer screen has yet to ravage your eyesight, and just allow a sliver of light to sneak through while viewing these beauties. The type might go fuzzy but the basic layout will remain so strong that it is dazzling.

The problem for the rest of the world was that we simply were not Swiss (there were a few like-minded Germans, sure, but the majority were in deep trouble.) It turned out that everything that seemed simple about this form of layout was not simple after all. It took a certain mindset and a great deal of restraint to design in this manner. It was also a tad boring, always following the rules. But you have to remember: you need to know the rules in order to break them.

It wasn't just design rules, either. The basic needs for producing a printed piece and the tight sequence of registration for a mechanical meant that designers needed to be tight craftsmen when it came to layout. Having items line up to invisible grid lines often meant lining them up to actual, drawn, non-repro blue lines on each layer or a base of illustration board. Taking this into consideration, you can see how "breaking" the grid was something that did not happen very often.

As printing became the main means of communication, these tenets of layout became the bedrock for organizing a page. Readability and navigation were greatly improved, and it became readily apparent when something had been assembled unprofessionally. Layout became much more akin to architecture as opposed to painting. This would not always hold true.

Graphic design runs in cycles, at least as far as I can tell, based on analyzing the publications that report on it. We go through "clean" years where the form stays tightly to the path paved for us by the Swiss. A certain four-letter organization relishes these phases. Just before we find ourselves bored to tears, a set of maverick designers (usually on a shoestring budget) will revolt and push us into a "messy" period. I love these times as the layouts are filled with complexity and reward detailed analysis. The multilayered type and imagery (not done with a computer, by the way, kids) of Vaughn Oliver, the counterculture flower-power imagery of the 1960s, Art Chantry's blown-out Xeroxes, right up to David Carson's deconstruction of the written word; the work of these designers engages us through challenging layout. There are just enough remnants of the rules there to make the breaking of them all the more impressive.

Both schools find many imitators, and the commonality of the masters of layout becomes apparent. It is hard work creating an engaging page, whether using a little or a lot of elements to do so. Few will truly emerge as owners of the form.

Courageous designers have stretched the very definition of what it means to lay out a page. My favorite "layout moments" are when the creator fashions a direction to make the medium work in new ways: Reid Miles smashing glass over his design and then photographing it, and Stefan Sagmeister having Martin Woodtli carve the "layout" into his skin and then snapping a pic come to mind. These organic 3-D designs displayed in 2-D fashion take "layout" to another world.

Another world is where layout is headed, by the way. As digital media emerges as the main means of communication, the organization of information has never been more important. If you thought the grid was important to the printed page, it is absolutely vital to the digital version. This form of design still has a long way to go, but I know successful layout will soon rule the day. I will be patiently waiting for it while I download my e-mails, as I reach my hand across the table to touch yours...

MARK KINGSLEY

The average breath cycle of a human being (inhalation and exhalation) lasts about three seconds, as does the average spoken phrase—no matter what the language may be.

Corporeality traps us within bodies, time, and history. It affects perception and consciousness, communication and understanding. The body and its senses act as filters between the self and the environment, with variations of interpretation and expression stemming from the combination of individual biology, context, errors, or random occurrences.

Simply put, style starts with the body. Each creative individual's style is uniquely their own: a result of the nervous system, blood chemistry, metabolism, eyesight, and every other ailment or constitutional element imaginable.

When we speak of style, we are referring to the method in which the inner state of the artist is conveyed to the larger world. A particular style is made up of the continuity of choices taken over time: size, proportion, color, composition, etc. Technical, geographic, or historical factors may spread stylistic elements from person to person, establishing a style in the broader sense of the word, but the idea of style stemming from method remains.

Preferences in the creation and reception of a work are better known as taste. This criterion, determined by sociological and intellectual judgments, was defined by Immanuel Kant as *sensus communis* (collective sense), or the "faculty of estimating what makes our feeling in a given representation... communicable without the mediation of a concept."

The categorization of style is taste. Taste establishes context; context creates difference. And difference—here/there, present/absent, now/then—is the fundamental building block of meaning. Thus, taste becomes an element of communication.

Genre is the abstract term referring to vague, sometimes arbitrary, groupings of context and subject. Styles can be the building blocks of genre, but generally aren't necessary to define a genre. For example, Ridley Scott's film *Blade Runner* incorporated specific clothing and hairstyles, voiceover exposition, and musical cues to evoke the film noir genre of the 1940s. Even without those stylistic indications, the ambiguity of the film's morality and narrative could place it in the film noir genre, regardless of the science-fiction setting. But their presence quickly telegraphs the director's intent, making the argument that these style cues help create the story.

Style, taste, and genre are all part of the designer's toolbox, as well as part of the designer's daily struggle. There are quite a few anecdotal reports of designers who become well known for a particular style (the design equivalent of winning the lottery) and then, several years later, find themselves out of fashion—the constant shift of popular taste. The struggle arises from the collision of the Renaissance idea of artist-as-interesting-character, standard art education encouragement to find one's uniqueness, and the vagaries of the marketplace.

The first significant art history, the 35th book of Pliny the Elder's *Natural History*, generally limited descriptions of style to an account of material innovations and items pictured—transparent drapery, teeth in an open mouth, etc. Pliny and his contemporaries praised artists like Apelles of Kos for their mimetic ability rather than their expression of an individual style.

Artists' personalities were not generally depicted until 1550, with the appearance of Giorgio Vasari's *Lives of the Most Excellent Painters, Sculptors, and Architects*. Vasari was an artist in the period known as Mannerism—from *maniera*, the Italian word for style. His *Lives* helped promote the opinion that artists needed to develop formal technique as well as a distinct point of view shaped by their personality and intellect. Based on his rather gossipy profiles of major figures like Michelangelo and Leonardo, a comparison could be drawn between the character of the artist, the quality of his work, and the refined sensibility of his patron.

Fast-forwarding 300 years, photography did the double duty of freeing art from the requirement of representation and speeding up the dissemination of stylistic developments. Now the focus was fully set on the difference between individual styles and the cult of artistic originality.

Like any other creative field, graphic designers need to balance the studio and the marketplace. The lifelong practice of developing one's craft and style occurs in the studio, while the marketplace is where one's style (and taste) conveys meaning. One learns from the other. Innovations from the studio have an effect on the marketplace, and the marketplace lets the designer know how his or her stylistic innovations are received. If they are effective, the designer gets more work.

Along with this cycle of expression and feedback, the designer also engages in a dialogue with history. Since various tastes help frame ideas, the appropriation of various styles from history, other cultures, or even fellow designers, becomes part of the designer's toolbox. As in everyday studio practice, the appropriation of outside style works best if attention is paid to the basics: intent, context, invoked sensibilities, and so on.

While it's easy to find an appealing formal device while flipping through a design magazine, the possibility exists that this solution will be little more than a decorative element. While that may be fine for some projects, if we take the position that graphic design is essentially a variation of storytelling, then we're not fulfilling our potential.

No, it's better to look outside graphic design history when researching or appropriating other styles. Many formal innovations were the result of technological invention, which in turn came from larger economic, scientific, and social developments. Trade with Asia and the Reformation begat movable type, scientific experimentation begat lithography, and the computer revolution begat PostScript. And at each step a Giambattista Bodoni, a Toulouse-Lautrec, or a David Carson exploited these innovations in the development of their own style. A style which was the product of their individual reaction to their particular place in time.

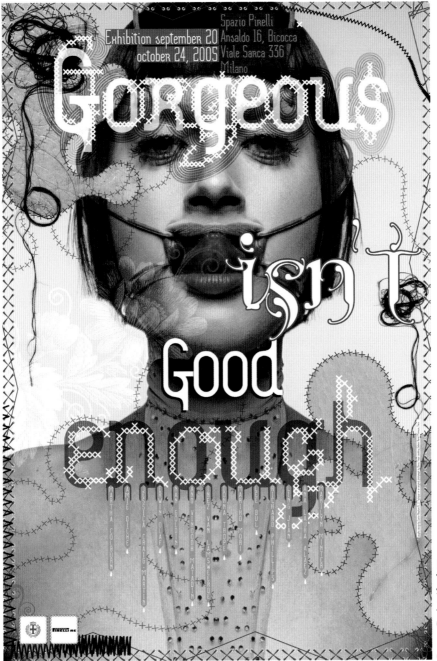

Exhibition september 20 october 24, 2005

Spazio Pirelli
Ansaldo 16, Bicocca
Viale Sarca 336
Milano

Gorgeous isn't Good enough

Image: Carine Abraham

PRINCIPLES OF THE CREATIVE PROCESS

Introduction

Graphic design is not just about graphic design. In today's visual landscape of sensory overload, there is no longer a mass market in which to target a product, logo, or package. Grant McCracken, the acclaimed author and anthropologist, has noted that while lifestyle typologies first expanded to three, then six, then nine, and then 12 typologies, there is now too much variation and we have reached categorical exhaustion. As a result, graphic design is ultimately only one part of the job of a graphic designer. Today, design must be the meticulously crafted balance of cultural anthropology, behavioral psychology, commerce, and creativity.

Graphic design must consider the cultural roots of any project. What we do in our culture—whether it is an obsession with celebrity, the weather, sports, fashion, or money—has a major impact on the way we view the world and our place in it. If we don't fundamentally understand the brain circuitry of our audience and really know what they are thinking and why they behave the way they do, we will not be able to solicit their imagination. We must understand the marketplace and how messaging impacts and influences perception.

The most delusional graphic design belief system is this: becoming a successful graphic designer is all about being an extraordinarily talented designer. It is not. Talent is only one part of the equation for a successful career in graphic design. In fact, in the field of professional graphic design, talent is simply what is considered "operational excellence" in business school. Talent is essentially a given, a point of entry. A career in graphic design brings with it the assumption that you have talent, and in isolation, talent will not guarantee success for any designer or design program.

Deep within every successful design program exists a cohesive plan for greatness, or a strategy. According to Harvard Business School professor Michael Porter, the definition of "strategy" is this: "Strategy is choosing to perform activities differently or to perform distinctly different activities than rivals." A strong and purpose-driven strategy can take away much of the subjectivity in evaluating graphic design, and if you can show how a program will be effective, rather than ask a client to "take your word," you will be far more effective in selling your creative ideas.

Ultimately, who we are as designers and what we believe in is as important as our ideas. Compelling graphic design solutions that are intrinsically intertwined with a clear, meaningful strategy are the key to creating extraordinarily effective and memorable communications. The following pages outline best practices in creating powerful visual strategy, how to test design solutions with market research, and how to bring your ideas to life with sound project management and a realistic understanding of the tenets of design production.

CHERYL SWANSON

VISUAL STRATEGY

Mood board: Toniq, LLC

Visual strategy did not exist as a marketing discipline 20 years ago, though it has become an essential element of brand success in the past decade. What is it and why is it so important now?

Visual strategy is the visual positioning of a brand in the marketplace. It is the foundation of a brand's visual representation across all media—advertising, packaging, web, promotions, and other forms of market presence—to ensure a consistent message to consumers. With a consistent message and focused visual expression, a brand has a much better chance of getting noticed in an increasingly complex, saturated marketplace and has, therefore, a much better chance of success.

Marketers started to realize the benefits of having a visual strategy for their brands in the mid-1990s, when the number of products in the average grocery store began to exceed 20,000 and media options began to proliferate. As we progressed into the twenty-first century, Americans were regularly exposed to 1,500–3,000 advertising messages daily from online, print, outdoor, and broadcast media. From 1999 to 2003, we created and stored more information than all the information produced since the beginning of mankind. Technology has fueled this information era and, because of it, we now process information 400 times faster than our Renaissance ancestors. In this survival-of-the-fastest lifestyle, we may be processing more information, but it is taking a toll on our bodies. Attention deficit disorder (ADD) is the neurological disorder of the decade, with two-thirds of us experiencing sleep disruptions and 90 percent of primary care visits due to stress-related ills such as acid reflux, ulcers, and depression. To survive this fast, constant, and sometimes debilitating information stream, we automatically edit out 85 percent of the information that comes our way. The information that penetrates these filters and is retained tends to be information that is symbolic, relevant to our lives, and meaningful intellectually and emotionally. It must engage our hearts, as well as our minds, to really be noticed.

Harnessing the visual sense can engage the mind and embrace the heart. Humans are a sight-driven species. Unlike our cats and dogs at home, who have heightened senses of smell, hearing, and vision, humans have 70 percent of their sensory receptors in their eyeballs, and 80 percent of what we learn about the world comes through our eyes. Additionally, we tend to remember symbols more readily and easily than we remember words. In the hierarchy of visual memory, humans remember colors first, shapes second (these can be three-dimensional shapes, geometric primitives, graphic shapes, or logos), numbers third, and words last. Yet throughout most of the history of marketing, brands have been developed with words and numbers only.

That was then...

Traditionally (and often so now), brand development was a numeric and written process stewarded by highly trained, linear-thinking MBAs. Consumer insights were often only quantitative and lifestyle trends were delivered via numbers and statistical analysis. A written positioning statement—defined as how the marketer wishes the brand to be perceived by consumers versus the competition—was the primary tool used to brief creative firms responsible for communicating a brand's message. Yet significantly, we all tend to have differing "mind's eye" visions of words—sometimes quite considerable differences. The word "youthful," for example, can evoke people as varied as young kids, teens, or active adults, or a state of being such as high-energy or radiant vibrance. To take another example, "blue" can evoke every hue from navy blue to cobalt to aqua to pale blue, and many variations in between. Consequently, when the various agencies—who have a majority of creative thinkers who process information in an associative, symbolic, nonlinear manner—were briefed in this written, linear manner, the visual interpretation of the brand differed across agencies and media. The brand story and resulting consumer brand experience was often fragmented rather than synergistic. These inconsistent interpretive choices end up like a game of "telephone," with an end result that is often less than optimal for the consistent impression of the brand.

To compound this issue, when advertising agencies, design firms, and other agencies presented creative solutions from these written briefs, the resulting meetings could often be antagonistic rather than a communicative partnership. The marketers—who had their own "mind's eye" vision of the brand's visual presence—often perceived the agency's interpretation as a misunderstanding of the positioning and the brief. Rounds of creative brainstorming would be conducted—at a great expenditure of money and time—to explore the "what ifs" of the positioning, with the agency trying to figure all the various ways in which the positioning could be brought to life, too often trying to second-guess the client. The client didn't always share the same vision, either; there was often dissent among the brand's management ranks about what the brand should look like.

This is now...

A bridge was needed to link the verbal/linear and the symbolic/associative processes of brand development; a way to translate the words into a visual zone or territory that brought to life the brand's essence and provided a visual foundation from which all agencies could build the brand's communications. In the mid-1990s, I developed one of the first visual positioning protocols to create that bridge.

The foundation for an effective visual strategy is a clear understanding of the consumer, their lifestyle, and the needs or desires met by the brand in order to create a compelling visual presence. It is imperative to transcend product attributes and "ladder up" to the emotional benefits people derive from the brand experience. We define those benefits as the quintessential qualities for which the consumer believes there is no substitute. Pepsi or Coca-Cola exemplify the passion consumers have for their respective brands; each brand is a cola, but is imbued with emotional qualities that surpass mere "cola-ness" by their respective consumer enthusiasts. Pepsi is youth, vitality, and "next generation," while Coca-Cola is "classic Americana" and consumers will not trade one for the other; it is these emotional or "higher order" qualities that transform a product into a brand.

The key element in connecting the consumer to these symbolic, higher order brand messages is the creation of a visual vocabulary that expresses the core essence, the fundamental personality, of the brand. This vocabulary is comprised of many elements, including:

COLOR PALETTE (hues, tones, tints, gradients)

TEXTURAL ELEMENTS (woods, metallics, plastics, stone, gloss, reflectivity, translucency)

MOVEMENT (blurs, vectors, directionals, geometries, dimension)

CONSUMER-RELEVANT VISUAL CUES (e.g. don't use someone young in age if expressing youthful as an attitude such as "zest for life")

CUES THAT CREATE DISTINCTION IN THE CATEGORY (these are "beyond the box" types of linkages that provide breakthrough appeal)

This vocabulary is then realized through a range of visual territories designed to clearly articulate the dimensions of the brand personality and the ways in which it may be brought to life. The vocabulary is intended to inform and inspire, not to be proscriptive or literal. It is not "design" in the ordinary or utilitarian sense of the term, though it employs the language of design to achieve many of its effects. These visual territories form the basis of an overall strategy that creates agreement internally, as well as with all agency partners, to ensure a focused consensus, because everyone is working from a common framework, speaking a common language, based on agreed strategic principles.

The end result is an integrated written and visual positioning, complete with sensory guidelines, used to create a clear, synergistic message across all media. This final dimensional positioning is a valuable tool as well in briefing agencies, internal audiences, and the business community.

While this recipe may seem more common sense than magic, it has yet to be consistently practiced after more than a decade of proven effectiveness. Still, when you move from the relative Babel of subjective brand interpretation to the strategic and symbolic dimension of visual positioning, with its ensuing rationale and brand consistency, it has certainly proved magic for those products and companies who are practicing it. And magically successful.

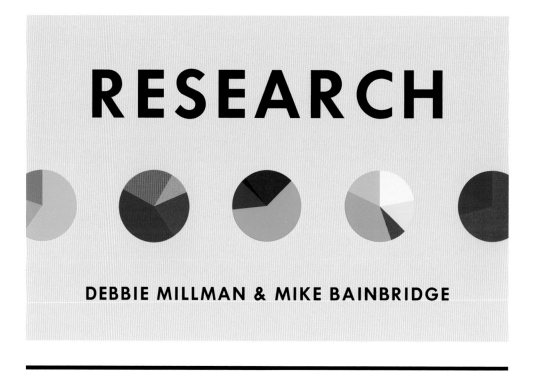

RESEARCH

DEBBIE MILLMAN & MIKE BAINBRIDGE

Back in the late 1800s, automobile maker Henry Ford remarked that if you'd questioned consumers about what they hoped for next in transportation, they would say that what they wanted was a faster and stronger horse. This was primarily due to the limits of our imagination as a population at the time. Culturally speaking, people are generally stymied by self-determined limits that hinder creation and invention. As a result, prior to the invention of the car, the preconceived boundaries of our collective imagination were constrained by notions of what seemed possible, tangible, and even logical. The idea of an "automobile" was as foreign and mysterious a concept then as time travel might seem to be now.

Henry Ford's commentary during the infancy of market research foreshadowed a sentiment about the discipline that is still very much alive today. Qualitative and quantitative market research often get a bad rap in the graphic design industry—and in the marketing world in general. Those that are vehemently against the practice argue that because consumers are generally uncomfortable with change, any type of research that probes something truly innovative or revolutionary will most likely scare people. Those that are skeptical will question the nature of the behavioral dynamics involved in artificial group settings. Even those who are merely dubious will admit that research can stifle creativity.

The golden rules of market research

1. Focus on testing communication effectiveness versus design appeal. Market research should be about perceptions, not preferences. And never ask if a piece of graphic design will influence a purchase decision; no self-respecting person will admit that they are so superficial as to be influenced this way—though we all are!

2. When testing, make allowances for familiarity. We are all generally more comfortable with what we know, and human beings, as a species, tend to be frightened of change.

3. Market research is an art, not a science. Try to investigate emotional connections and design sensibilities. Avoid an over-dependence on numerical imperatives.

4. Focus on what consumers like about the brand or product first, then ask them to focus on what a design is communicating about the brand or product in general. Try to avoid asking consumers to explain why they like what they like in specific design terms.

5. More is definitely merrier. Never test designs in isolation. Let consumers see designs alongside other designs or next to competitors. This makes it easier to respond through comparing and contrasting.

6. The big no-no: never ask consumers how they would improve a design; they're not design experts and you want their reactions, not their solutions.

Questioning consumers about their lives and choices first began in the USA back in 1790 with the first census, which was initiated primarily to determine voting demographics. It wasn't until 1920, when Procter & Gamble executives went door-to-door asking American housewives for their opinions on new products and packaging, that the modern age of market research really began. But it was in 1930 that the discipline truly took shape, when social scientists A.C. Nielsen and George Gallup started quantitative testing and surveying. In 1950 the first qualitative testing began by getting a highly targeted audience of consumers with a similar set of needs or concerns to understand their motivation, purchase behavior, and attitude development within a particular frame of reference. These pioneering market researchers used psychology, anthropology, creativity, and sociology to study a new topic: why people buy the stuff that they buy. It's not unfair to say that all modern advertising sprang from this groundbreaking work.

Cut to the present day and we find that Malcolm Gladwell, author of runaway anthropological bestsellers *Blink* and *The Tipping Point*, has called for the abolition of focus groups. He contends that because human beings cannot rationalize initial impressions, it is both misleading and dangerous to ask people to explain what they like and why they like it. Documented examples of this come from far and wide, but the most convincing are the market research studies conducted prior to the launch of New Coke and Absolut Vodka. New Coke was considered an unequivocal slam dunk in taste tests against Classic Coke but was subsequently a failure of epic proportions when it went to market. Conversely, the Absolut Vodka bottle design was universally panned in focus groups. A courageous Michel Leroux, then the brand manager of the new vodka, pressed for its launch and the brand set international sales records. The Absolut bottle is now considered a contemporary design icon. So when the demand for validating design solutions is so strong, yet research is seemingly so fraught with pitfalls, what is a designer to do?

There is a group of brand consultants and cultural anthropologists that believes that it is not the actual research itself that's the problem. It is rather about how research is often misused, what type of design concepts and stimulus are tested, and how data is analyzed. When used correctly, research shouldn't stifle creativity but offer designers stronger inspiration and focus.

There are a wide variety of research techniques that can have merit for designers, but like any techniques, there are different tools, stimuli, and surveying mechanisms that are appropriate for each purpose. There is not, repeat not, one correct way to test design.

The following are some of the mainstays of modern market research. With each is included the advantages, the challenges, and the bottom line.

Ethnographic research

Some of the best design research does not involve testing actual design at all. In fact, it is usually conducted before any conceptual work begins.

Ethnography is the branch of anthropology that provides scientific descriptions of individual human societies. Ethnographic research involves rigorous one-on-one conversations and observations with consumers within their everyday surroundings—at home, at work, shopping, in a bar, and so forth. This helps marketers and designers understand consumers on a much deeper level than any other qualitative research technique. For a few hours (or days!) you get to see the world through the consumer's eyes, observe the context in which design operates in their lives, and witness first hand their current aesthetic sensibilities. You get an in-depth view of their homes and their choices. Good ethnographers don't ask consumers to play a designer or brand expert, they are simply asked to be themselves. This provides a complex and rich picture of creative sensibilities. Further, the insights gleaned are most valuable to developing a design that will emotionally connect and delight. Many marketers have embraced the ethnographic research technique both as a panacea to their frustrations with focus groups and because it gets much closer to consumer truths.

THE ADVANTAGES

- It brings you much closer to "reality"
- It provides deeper profiling of consumers: lifestyles, brand relationships, design sensibilities, shopping dynamics
- It unearths truths through observation as well as discussion
- It is particularly good for sensitive topics

THE CHALLENGES

- It is time-consuming
- You often get limited sample sizes
- There is limited client involvement in the actual research

THE BOTTOM LINE

- Ethnographic research gives you the ability to comprehend consumers on a deeper level, thus allowing for a better understanding of their imagination through design

Focus groups

Many marketers agree with Malcolm Gladwell that focus groups are dangerous, but this is less because of the forum itself, and more because of the ways in which such groups are abused. Clients are often apt to say, "Let's let the focus groups tell us what consumers want." Then a design strategy team will be required to question a rogue set of amateur strangers to come to a consensus in two hours about a marketing and design strategy they know nothing about. It is fraught with difficulties. Put another way, if the Absolut Vodka brand team had simply given consumers what they thought they wanted, the design icon would not have made it to market. Instead, the research findings taught them that the design they had was likely to disrupt and challenge the status quo—and that was in sync with the original strategy.

Focus groups are an efficient forum when identifying what design concepts are communicating on an intuitive level. But beware: this is where facilitators can sometimes force consumers to rationalize their responses or be the arbiter of what's right and wrong. Instead, their reactions should be used as one of the filters to help the designer and brand teams understand which designs will create the desired effect and delight the most.

THE ADVANTAGES

- They can give quick and controlled feedback
- They are best used to explore broader conceptual themes versus tight executions
- Design can be utilized to stimulate emotions, not to arrive at solutions

THE CHALLENGES

- They usually take place in an unnatural environment (one-way mirrored room)
- Respondents often say what they think you want to hear, not what they really feel
- It is tempting to treat consumers as if they were art directors and experts
- Focus groups are often perceived as old-fashioned

THE BOTTOM LINE

- Try and keep this stalwart technique fresh, and experiment with new approaches

Quantitative eye tracking

Quantitative market research is the systematic attempt to define, measure, and report on the relationships between various elements. In design it is used to essentially compare one design to another in a very specific environment. Eye tracking is simply the tracking of the pupil as it moves across an image. Eye-tracking technology was pioneered over 30 years ago by Elliott Young at Perception Research Systems and is now the leading technology for measuring how humans "see" products. Eye-tracking technology is highly effective at measuring the way consumers navigate a design (what they look at first, what they pause at longer, what they go back to and study again). It is also particularly good for testing impact in packaging design. It is can be considered accurate as long as both the current and new design are being tested under exactly the same circumstances and with a significant number of consumers (at least 100 to 150 of any one target demographic). It is also a useful measure of how a final design is going to stand out in a retail environment. The danger lies in the obvious: it becomes easy to evaluate these results in isolation and not consider the total context in which the design may be launched. For example, will the brand or product be supported by promotions, advertising, and point of purchase? It is important to consider the results of this type of testing as one of the filters for decision-making rather than the final arbiter.

THE ADVANTAGES

- Marketers often believe the following: that which is not measured is not fully valued!
- Eye tracking is significantly more sophisticated than any other type of quantitative research
  - Noting: who sees what
  - Speed of noting: how quickly they see each element
  - Re-examination: who returns to look at something again
- You get multi-dimensional measurement: aesthetic appeal, product expectations, imagery, shelf impact, purchase intent, etc.
- You receive numerical and projectable ratings
- It is an excellent test of impact and alienation

THE CHALLENGES

- It is sometimes used as "go/no go" decision-maker rather than a diagnostic tool to guide a final decision, and this can be short-sighted
- It cannot realistically project sales impact

THE BOTTOM LINE

- Educate your researchers, as design is a small part of their business
- Use it to inform, and not dictate

Online testing

Online testing provides feedback from a large group of people relatively quickly and cost-effectively. But like all research techniques, it has drawbacks. There is considerably less control over how respondents can react to the aesthetic quality of what they are seeing and there is limited scope for real-time dialogue with consumers. There is also a dependency on respondents being honest about whom they "say" they are. (Watch out, you might have 18-year-old male miscreants logging on to your test for menopausal hormone replacements!)

THE ADVANTAGES

* It casts a wide net
* It is time- and cost-efficient as well as flexible
* It is kind of "cool"

THE CHALLENGES

* There is often a misconception about speed; it is not really that fast
* There is a limit to how long respondents will stay involved online
* There is no way to ensure the purity of polling sample
* There are inherent issues with quality control; design subtleties can be lost on screen

THE BOTTOM LINE

* This is a mode of testing that has yet to be truly embraced by the design community

The road ahead

There's almost nothing more demoralizing for a designer than witnessing a bunch of non-designer consumers ripping apart their hard work. But if you are able to step back for a moment and watch the spontaneous enthusiasm and delight that great design can elicit in a consumer, it can ignite passion in a truly profound and deeply resonating way. Ultimately, it is important to remember this: market research does not determine good design. Designers must design the work before it goes to research. However, in today's risk-averse corporate world, it is unlikely that market research will be going away any time soon. But take comfort in the quantifiable fact that when used correctly, the insight it provides can be an amazing springboard for creativity.

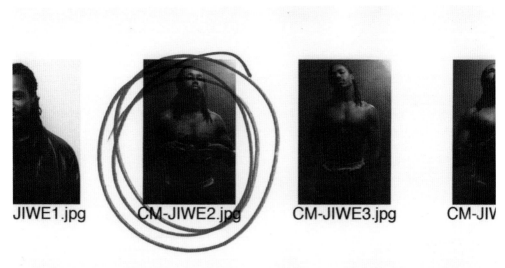

JIWE1.jpg   CM-JIWE2.jpg   CM-JIWE3.jpg   CM-JIV

WORKING WITH IMAGERY

JOHN FULBROOK

As an art director and designer, I have been working with imagery for many years. Experience is key when heading down the path of choosing or shooting a photograph, or commissioning an illustration to help solve a design problem. I wish someone had pulled me aside a long time ago and whispered a few tips in my ear to enlighten me on how to successfully work with this medium. I had to learn about working with imagery the hard way. To spare you the agony, here are 10 important considerations to keep in mind when working with imagery.

1. What is the purpose of the imagery?

Editors and designers often choose images based on their power and individual merit. When designing a comprehensive piece, this is not a good way to work. Instead, ask yourself the following questions: What you want the image to do for the overall project? Do you want the image to get special attention? What emotion does it need to evoke? How will the support type and other required information work with the imagery? I see so many projects designed where the image was wonderful, but did not accommodate the typography or support the overarching message of the piece. Keep the final project in mind and make sure the image feels cohesive.

2. Remember juxtaposition

The image of a turkey can mean many things, but if you caption it with the words "George Bush," you will invoke a very particular message. Keep this in mind, as the combination of language and imagery can change the context of the image or text in isolation. Careful juxtaposition will help you accurately convey a specific message.

3. When adding type to images, make sure your type relates to that particular image

Young designers generally use standard type layouts that have no premeditated relation to the chosen image. A good exercise you can undertake to test the relevance of your image is this: can you insert a picture of your butt into the layout? If nothing changes and the type works as well with any imagery, then you are not working with the image properly.

4. Respect great photography and illustration

A good way to keep photographers and illustrators happy is to take great care in how you use their images. If you need a blue sky, try to art-direct it into the image, rather then relying on Photoshop to enhance it. Also, try not to dramatically change cropping, as the image was likely cropped that way for a reason. Moreover, if you need an image to be a certain size, factor this into your art direction. Choose images that will be complemented by the layout you have designed, rather than fighting or competing with it. Chances are, if you use giant pink type over the main face on an image, then crop it five times and make it a darker blue, a photographer or illustrator will resent you for trashing their beautiful image.

5. Take a safety shot

I am a firm believer in really going for exactly what you want on a photo shoot. Push the limits, break the rules, provoke and change the way people see. However, I think a good art director will know both what the client wants and what the company wants. While you might try to push these parameters, it is important to keep all of your bases covered. Even when I hire the best possible photographer and we see eye to eye on the concept and style of the shoot, I always build in several safety options that I am completely confident my client will love. This approach has saved me from blowing budgets and losing clients many times.

6. Try to avoid stock

There are so many talented photographers and illustrators willing to work for reasonable fees that I try to use new imagery whenever possible. However, when clients ask for 20 different iterations, I will use stock for conceptual sketching and storyboarding. Then I will present the layouts with a sample of the photographers or illustrators I want to work with. This gets the client excited about the potential of creating a new piece of art for the project, but allows them to visualize what the work will look like. This practice can aid in the successful execution of a great image with minor alteration. But remember, if you make your sketch look "too good," you might be asked to use that and skip the shoot. You don't want that to happen!

7. Credit photographs properly

Have you ever noticed that the credit for the *Mona Lisa* is "© Corbis?" It doesn't matter if you are using a great stock photo from Magnum or if you hire a photographer or illustrator that you know, always remember to double-check the credit line.

8. Don't expect duplication

Great photographers and illustrators are artists who are continually bringing something new or fresh to their work. Recognize a nuance, mood, or idiosyncrasy in their work that you love and would like to work with, but leave room for something exciting and different to happen. Nothing is worse then asking an artist to duplicate something they have already done.

9. Build relationships

Some of my best design work is due to the strong relationships I have with the artists I work with. Remember: win the war and not the battle. If you build good bonds with photographers and illustrators, it will be easier for you to ask for a favor when you need one. If you follow this advice and respect your photographers and illustrators, you will get twice the effort back in the results.

10. Show the love!

I was recently on an airplane and saw a listing in the *Sky Mall* magazine for an inexpensive in-home photo studio. I have also heard endless stories about how good digital cameras are now and how nonprofessionals can shoot most photographs on their own. Resist! If you have a budget, give the commission to a professional artist, photographer, or illustrator. Chances are they have considerably more experience than you do in their specialized medium. Show the love, and pay it forward. You will undoubtedly get better design as a result.

SATORU WAKESHIMA

ACCOUNT MANAGEMENT AND WORKFLOW

Before I started in this business, I never knew it existed. I didn't study graphic design in school, so it wasn't something I knew I wanted to do. After graduating from college, I wanted to get into advertising—years of watching *Bewitched*, *Thirtysomething*, and countless other television shows had led me to believe that people actually got paid to sit around and come up with "big ideas" for ad campaigns. I could do that. So when a family friend was able to arrange an interview with one of the larger agencies in Manhattan, I leapt at the opportunity, but was quickly disappointed when I discovered that all the entry-level positions were filled. There was, however, an opening with their graphic design agency. The criterion for my decision was simple: I needed a job. So I took it.

Fast-forward 20 years and I am still in this business. I'm not a graphic designer and I am not employed by an advertising agency. I work in a field called brand consulting, or branding. At the firm where I currently work, one of my primary responsibilities is overseeing the account management team. This role in brand consulting or graphic design is also commonly referred to as "client services," "project management," "account services," or "account group." Simply stated, the role of account management is to manage the process; form, build, and maintain solid client relationships; and provide sound advice.

As the manager of project process, you are a ringmaster of sorts, bringing a variety of resources together, communicating with them all, and making sure they're communicating. You are managing all activity from start to finish, and all the financial matters in between. As keeper of the client relationship, your role is to build trust; establish a partnership that is fair and equitable for both client and agency; and to be the friendly, always ready, always eager-to-help face and voice that is there to reassure the client that every aspect of a project will be handled well. Lastly, while "providing sound advice" doesn't sound like a description of a professional role in a creative agency, it quite accurately describes what is perhaps the most intangible role of account management: consulting. The intrinsic role of consultant includes providing clients with thoughts, options, tools, and solutions to their problems based on your experience and expertise as a design professional.

Managing process

To understand an account person's role, one must first understand the basic process of a typical graphic design project. Regardless of agency, most projects follow a process that includes different phases of activity, for example:

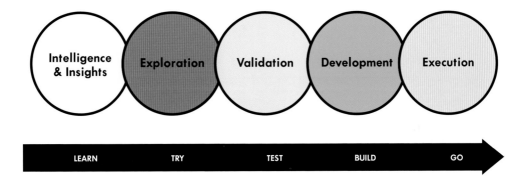

While agencies will use intelligent-sounding terms to describe (and sell) their processes, in essence they are all doing the same thing: learning, trying, testing, building, and going.

LEARNING: All projects start with the gathering of information—about the brand, marketplace, target audience, competitors, and similar brands inside and outside the category, etc. You may need to conduct research to gain information you don't have.

TRYING: After examining all the information, you start to form hypotheses and explore ideas for anything from the brand's positioning, name, graphics, cost, retail execution, or all of these. These ideas are then brought to life in some tangible form in order to proceed to the next step.

Testing: Before a company decides to invest significant dollars to execute an idea, they'll typically conduct research to determine the idea's appeal, effectiveness, difference from competitors, or relevance. Companies and their agencies use research as a tool to help determine which ideas are working best and why, to narrow down and focus ideas, and to guide further development.

Building: Once an idea has been selected as the idea with which to move forward, it needs to be "built." Building the idea might involve refining or modifying in an effort to make it the best it can be.

Going: Lastly, one must finalize all details necessary to execute an idea. Whether this stage involves creating reproducible artwork, mechanical files, final renderings, or a launch event, an idea is only as good as its execution.

The following is an outline of the design phases involved in a typical project:

Phase 1: Design planning (learning)

Phase 2: Design exploration (trying)

Phase 3: Design refinement (trying)

Phase 4: Design development (trying)

Phase 5: Qualitative research (testing)

Phase 6: Post-research refinement (building)

Phase 7: Quantitative research (more testing)

Phase 8: Design finalization (building)

Phase 9: Artwork and mechanicals (going)

Managing a project involves the collection, organization, and transfer of information. Clients provide information, which the account person translates into comprehensive and concise terms for the creative and production teams. Inevitably, there are questions, which the account person gathers and conveys to the client. This back and forth exchange of information may sound simple, and it generally is, but it requires organization and attention to detail. There are timelines to create and maintain, proposals and estimates to be written, budgets to manage, and deadlines to meet. As the account person is responsible for all of this, they lead and drive the process.

The most challenging aspect of an account person's role is managing time. Eighty percent of the world's problems can be solved with more time. However, there will inevitably be situations in which you simply cannot obtain or create more time. Herein lies the ultimate challenge for the account person. The phases of a project require a finite amount of time. While you may be able to modify certain design activities to accommodate an aggressive schedule at some point, it simply cannot be done any faster. And yet clients will urge you to make it happen, and when they do, you'd better have a good relationship...

Forming and maintaining a client relationship

As the primary point of contact between client and agency, it is the account person's responsibility to form, maintain, and build lasting relationships with clients. Strong client relationships are founded on two very basic elements: trust and partnership. Design projects are actually just one of the many tasks on your client's plate at any given time. If you are able to instill confidence and trust in your client, you'll give them one less thing to worry about.

One important factor in gaining such trust is frequent, detailed communication. An account manager who proactively keeps their clients updated on project timing, progress, budgets, etc. will circumvent questions, worry, and paranoia. But trust is earned, not granted, and it is your ability to consistently deliver on promises of quality of work, cost, and timing efficiency, that will earn a client's trust over time. A big part of earning trust is also letting clients know when they're asking for the impossible.

Many years ago, I worked on a design project for a major brewing company to introduce a new brand. My client, the marketing director, told me that he needed refinements to a design and 300 three-dimensional mockups created in a week. After checking with my team, I confirmed my suspicions that this was quite impossible and called him to let him know that we'd have to discuss alternative approaches, as there simply wasn't enough time to accomplish what he'd requested. He was furious, insisted it could be done, and if I couldn't get it done, he'd find someone that could. Frustrated and upset, I went back to my team to ask if there was any way to make it happen, short of changing the deliverables—there wasn't.

After cooling off, I called my client back to discuss what was possible, given the timeframe. I got his voicemail and against my better judgment, I told him what I really thought: the timing was impossible and rather than telling him what he wanted to hear and then disappointing him by missing the deadline and delivering poor-quality work, I told him what the realities were to get it done right and that we were doing everything we could to make it happen as quickly as possible. I asked him to call me at home that evening to discuss things further (I give most clients my home phone number—few actually use it). He did call me at home that night and apologized. He said he completely respected my calling him out on an impossible and unreasonable request and further respected that I wasn't willing to compromise our, or his, standards. I earned his trust that day and we enjoyed a great relationship for many years.

Partnership is the result of trust and mutual respect between two parties. It requires each to treat one another fairly, provide some degree of commitment, and have a relationship that is mutually beneficial. Clients pay agencies to do good work. Agencies do good work to get paid and get more work. But a partnership means more than an agreement of dollars and cents—it's about fairness, honesty, and making each other look good, so that everyone wins.

Providing sound advice

This last topic is perhaps the most ambiguous and difficult to describe, because what I'm really referring to is consulting. As with anything else, people seek advice from experts—people who have extensive knowledge and experience in a specific field. Clients seek the expertise of agencies for their knowledge and experience in graphic design, equity evaluation, visual asset management, portfolio segmentation, innovation, cultural and design trends, ethnography, and so forth. A consultant must be able to provide guidance (advice) on a host of topics at any given moment. While much of this quite simply comes from years of experience, it is the ability to draw from one's experience and connect the dots of relevancy between one design situation and another that makes a good consultant great. This ability to advise "on the fly" is difficult to teach. I use the words advise and advice, not opine, as anyone can give their opinion, but few can pull it off as an "expert" opinion. As such, it's a very fine line between complete and utter BS and consulting, and unfortunately, for many, the line wears thin.

Why would you want to do this?

I've described what an account person does and in turn, what I look for when hiring one: organizational skills, people skills, and consulting skills. So why would anyone want to do such a thing, let alone make a career of it? People that work in this capacity do so because they have an inherent fascination with design, process, and management. What makes one design preferred over another? How do competing products speak in completely different languages to the same audience? These questions are endlessly fascinating to the account person, and discovering the answers with a client even more so.

A person in an account management role in the design business has the opportunity to work on a variety of projects, each with unique challenges. They collaborate and interact with other creative and strategic minds and form lasting relationships with clients and colleagues that often span lifetimes. They are challenged with solving problems from unique perspectives and design approaches. They work in an exciting industry that is constantly evolving, yet respectful and deeply influenced by its history. And while they may be stressed, work long hours, and need more sleep, they are never, ever bored.

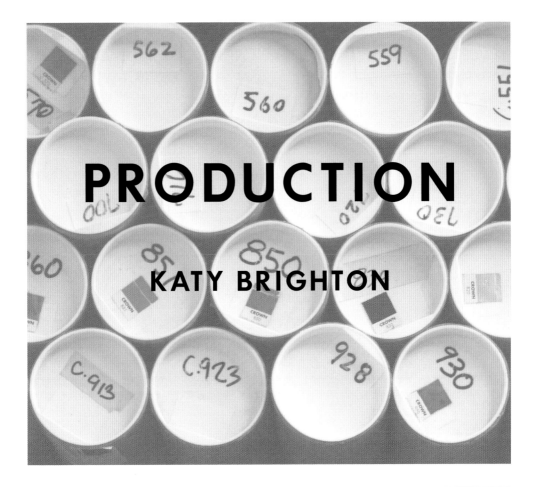

PRODUCTION

KATY BRIGHTON

Today, production means many things, and is continuously being redefined. Simply put, production is everything that needs to happen to a design before it is produced. Not so long ago, trained experts at a prepress house, separator, or printer handled the production process. Prepress professionals took care of everything from color separations and retouching, to trapping and typesetting. More often than not, a designer could never be certain what to expect, and would hope for the best.

Welcome to the digital age. Computers have revolutionized design. Suddenly the designer has more control over the process, making design more challenging and complex, with constantly changing technologies and techniques. Now a designer is required to make well-informed decisions utilizing their knowledge of the production process. This understanding of production will separate a fabulous design from a fabulous endeavor.

Getting what you want

My design is finished—now what? In the beginning, visualize the end. Develop clear and precise thinking from the outset. Be present at every step of the process to communicate and preserve your design vision—you are best suited to communicate your intention. Know what questions to ask in order to manage your expectations, and those of your client, when communicating with separators and printers. Develop a relationship with your printer and separator to resolve any potential issues that may arise. Involve the printer early in the creative process so that your design will not exceed any limitations or capabilities. These partnerships will prevent catastrophes on press and avoid any disappointment or embarrassment, ultimately yielding exactly the results you hope for.

Understanding the basics

Knowing the options and what is possible will facilitate communication. Gain an understanding of industry standards. Identify the best printing process for the job and familiarize yourself with these methods. Then choose a printer based on reputation, experience, up-to-date equipment, reliability, and availability. The main printing techniques are:

OFFSET LITHOGRAPHY, commonly called offset, is characterized by soft, smooth transitions of colors and crisp type. Offset can usually print up to eight colors on variable thicknesses and textures of paper stocks, and is used mostly to print magazines, newspapers, catalogs, and packaging.

FLEXOGRAPHY, or flexo, is the least expensive of the printing processes. It is distinguished by saturated color, and sharp breaks in gradient tints and vignettes. Flexo presses can usually print up to 10 colors, on paper or flexible film, to produce shrinkwraps, juice cartons, potato-chip bags, cereal boxes, yogurt containers, and newspaper inserts.

ROTOGRAVURE is portrayed by strong saturated colors and slightly ragged type. It is capable of printing 10 or more colors on transparent and flexible films. Gravure is also ideal for printing cartons, including die-cutting, embossing, and foil stamping, which can be done in-line on the press.

LETTERPRESS is known for sharp, crisp printing and grainy images, with gradient tints producing hard edges where color drops off. This process is used mostly for short-run printing such as announcements, invitations, and stationery.

SCREEN PRINTING is a unique short-run process that prints on almost any surface. Both solid and halftone color can be printed. This process is used for posters, labels, wallpaper, and textiles such as shower curtains and upholstery. Screen printing can also be done on wood, leather, glass, metal, ceramic materials, and plastics.

DIGITAL PRINTING, also referred to as on-demand printing, is gaining popularity. This process, likened to an oversize copier, is particularly successful for designs that require short runs, short schedules, and variable data, such as direct mail.

Bells and whistles

You've found a printer and have chosen your substrate and assigned colors. Now comes the fun part, the myriad of decisions that will need to be made to add the finishing touches to your design:

A COATING is an emulsion, varnish, or lacquer applied over the printed or unprinted surface of paper to protect it or to provide added shine.

EMBOSSING is an image pressed in relief to produce a raised effect. Conversely, the opposite process, debossing, yields a depressed image.

FOIL STAMPING is the application of foil to paper where a heated die is stamped onto the foil, making it adhere to the surface and leaving the design of the die on the paper. Foil stamping can be combined with embossing to create a more striking three-dimensional image.

DIE-CUTTING is the process of cutting specified shapes in paper.

SCORING is impressing or indenting a line into paper, to make folding easier and to prevent paper from cracking when it's folded.

FOLDING is usually done by machines and is not an exact science; a certain tolerance is needed that allows for variation as the paper shifts.

BINDING is the use of thread, staples, wire, glue, or other agents to collect sections into books, brochures, and pamphlets. There are dozens of types of binding. Which one you choose will depend on the number of pages, paper weight, and how the book will be used.

Making it happen

Design would not exist without production—production is design anticipated. Every step has been contemplated and every scenario considered. Relationships have been developed and some problems have been avoided, while others have been recognized as opportunities—bravo! The journey toward preserving design integrity from beginning to end needs only to commence with an informed designer.

PRINCIPLES
WITHIN DISCIPLINES

Introduction

According to Webster's dictionary, "change" means the following: to cause to be different; to change the spelling of a word or to give a completely different form or appearance; to transform. More often than not, human beings see change as risky and a threat to security. In fact, research suggests that people will actively fight or resist any new direction in their work unless they are absolutely convinced that this change will benefit them. In addition to fearing change, people fear a loss of security with new environments and new opportunities.

Almost synonymous with the fear of change is the fear of failure. Many people feel worried and anxious when they even consider undertaking something new, for fear of making a mistake. This fear is so overwhelming that any change at all will create a sense of dread and pessimism. Yet, at its core, graphic design is full of change. Design not only ignites external change; there are also endless paths that can be taken within the field of graphic design to inspire change.

Since the prehistoric days of cave drawings, human beings have been compelled to communicate and record events, discoveries, knowledge, and ideas via visual iconography. And from the day that Johannes Gutenberg invented printing from movable type, graphic design has been evolving, morphing, and changing. Each century has produced awe-inspiring new developments, including the two-dimensional mass-produced poster, the circulated periodical, the decorative book cover, the yearly corporate financial report, the designed three-dimensional product package and container, highway signage, experiential museum exhibits, environmental graphics, and the moving imagery of television and film, not to mention the potential of the internet. One fundamental truth has remained consistent throughout: we are driven to mark our existence.

Every design created has the potential to get swept up into the historical sequence of design that precedes and follows it. As a result, the condition of graphic design reflects and records the condition of our culture. Designers now have the capability to be an inspiration to our culture—no contribution can be excluded from this effort. This includes pet food, ballot forms, annual reports, propaganda posters, even breath mints. Everything that designers create can be approached with this sense of urgency. If not, we dilute the power to communicate what is occurring in our culture.

The following pages showcase some of the world's greatest graphic designers and present examples of their work in numerous disciplines within the field of graphic design. Each case study features the professional creative journey undertaken by each designer, as well as personal thoughts, anecdotes, and lessons learned along the way. In addition, each study includes an overview of the individual design process, the creative decision-making and inventive practices that define each designer's uniquely original voice. My hope is that these case studies will prove that the far-reaching discipline of graphic design has more impact on our culture than any other creative medium.

PROJECT

The Peace Project

DESIGNER

Josh Chen, Chen Design

CLIENT

Self-Published

The Peace Project began when my staff at Chen Design realized we hadn't completed a self-promotional piece for some time. In our research, we thought about everything from a comprehensive listing of nonprofit groups, to an environmentally and socially conscious "gift catalog" of sorts.

Eventually, we stumbled upon a site for the Nuclear Age Peace Foundation—wagingpeace.org—which proffered a list enumerating "One hundred ideas for creating a more peaceful world," compiled by the foundation's president, David Krieger. The list encouraged visitors to take it and make it their own, to distribute as they saw fit, in order to further the cause of peace in the world. We immediately saw the visual potential in this, though we had no clue how intimately involved we would become.

Our first step was to make the list our own, as per Mr. Krieger's instructions, and we executed this by augmenting the content with our own contributions. This gave us a deeper sense of ownership, and endowed the list with a life of its own, making it more accessible

66.

Volunteer

time at an

afterschool

program

to people. The entire process was collaborative and organic—we worked to illustrate each other's ideas, organize the content, and figure out the exact shape the piece was going to take.

We like to begin with a visual toolbox. We collect as many examples of photography, found art, type, and design as we can find, withholding judgment on each piece's inherent value and appropriateness. The Peace list was straightforward and simple, on the dangerous border of becoming trite, so we had to make sure that the illustrations attributed to each idea would be as rich and, perhaps, as unrelated as possible. For instance, advice such as "Be honest," or "Say 'I love you,'" could come across as ordinary and predictable—invoking a bored response from the reader. We wanted each spread to be visually ambitious and highly conceptual. Since the text already spoke for itself, the illustration needed to step outside the words, to transcend meaning, to transport the reader into planes of higher thought and emotion. Abstract, obtuse, sophisticated, and stylized connections to the subject matter were not only encouraged but, in fact, required.

Project beginnings

We put together a preview of the project, in order to pitch it to various publishing houses. *100 Ways to Promote Peace* was an overlong title, but we felt it was necessary to define the project from square one. It took the form of a set of five postcards that were sent out as our 2002 year-end holiday greeting. An intriguing outer packaging ensured that people would take notice of the piece— vying for attention in the midst of the holiday mail flurry is always a tremendous challenge. Inside the glassine envelope one found a set of postcards held together by a rubber band. The cards expressed sentiments that were timely, given the events of the war in Iraq—for example: Idea 10, "Erase a border in your mind," or Idea 29, "Oppose all weapons of mass destruction."

Once I took the plunge and decided to self-publish the book, we had little more than a month to create the design. We were about 40 percent toward completion, and the majority of the book came together in October and November. Eight of us worked on the project, four of whom I dubbed the "Distinguished CDA alumni,"

Nov 2, 2003

Dear Dave,

Too much time has passed, and we didn't part on good terms. Much of this is my fault. I was angry, and blamed you for what happened. It took me a long time to realize that our friendship means too much to me to have it end like this. I know you didn't intend to hurt me,

or Jessica for that matter (she has ~~been~~ since left, and taken the cat with her). For what it's worth, I forgive you. I forgive you for everything. I sincerely hope you forgive me too....

I just want my friend back.

Love, Tracy

FORGIVE SOMEONE FROM YOUR PAST

ers and illustrators who continue to work with us today.
ector, Jennifer Tolo Pierce, and I worked on the bulk of
k. Zachariah O'Hora, a terrific illustrator, is also a member
'DA pack.

d design directions from client presentations were
sources for the project. It was fun to pull them out of
es, and regain the inspiration and motivation to do
ing new with them.

All illustrations are designer's visual representation of a specific "idea" from The Peace Project.

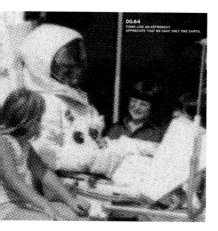

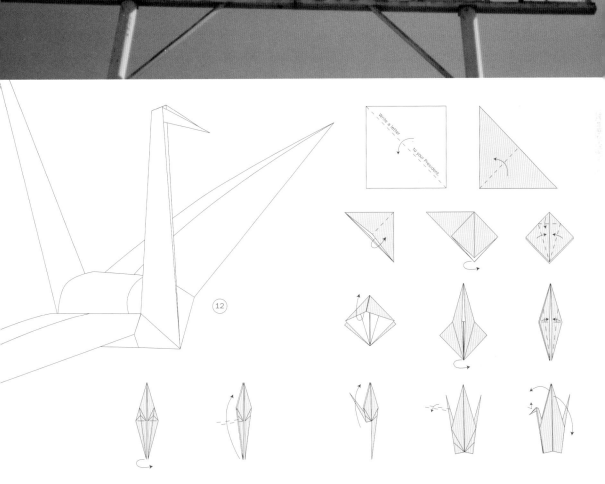

BREATHE DEEPLY

Write a letter to your President

12

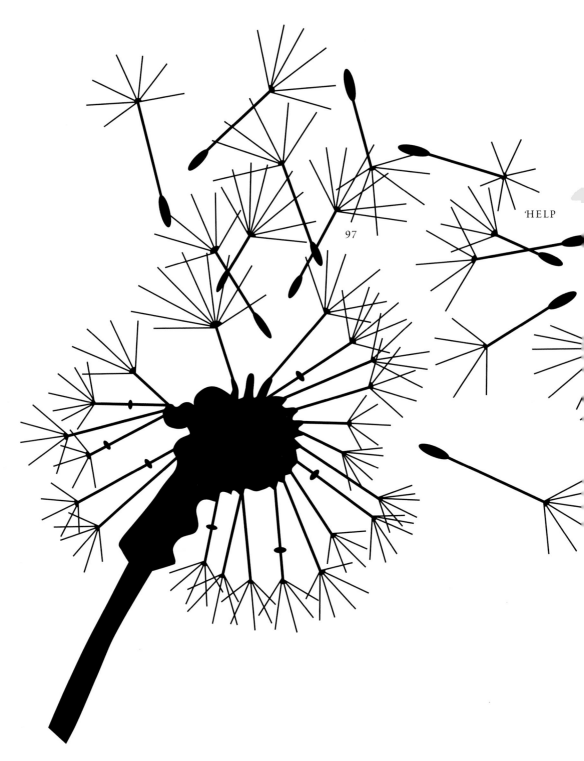

HELP

97

THE ESSENTIAL PRINCIPLES OF GRAPHIC DESIGN

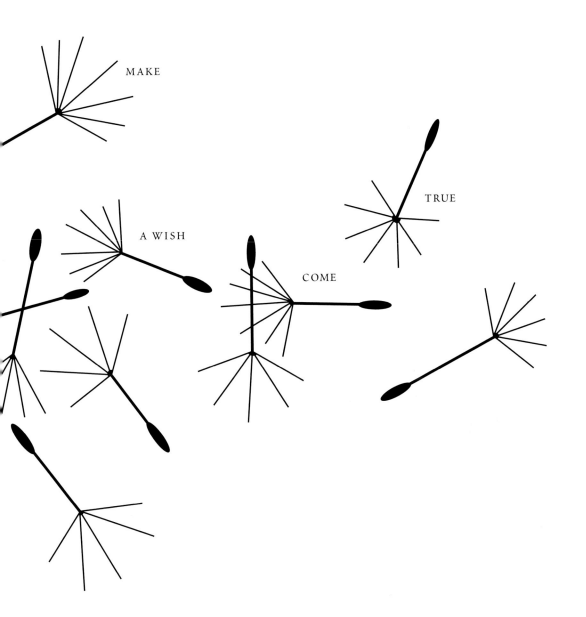

MAKE

A WISH

COME

TRUE

BOOK JACKET DESIGN

PROJECT

The Verificationist

DESIGNER

John Gall

CLIENT

Vintage Books

I employ two methodologies when designing book covers. I always make sure to read the manuscript, so that I can come up with a solid concept, then I gather visuals and go to it. There isn't a stage where I sketch, but there is a lot of tortuous pondering. Other times I might borrow some elements from the book and translate them into visuals. It's a roundabout way of working, but it often yields unexpected results. The designing of the cover itself is the easiest part. What is most difficult is the approval process, and the slow-death-by-tweaking book designers often have to deal with.

This is how I took the beautifully designed Knopf jacket for *The Verificationist* and turned it into a Vintage paperback. The original hardcover design was created by Carol Carson Devine. It is a wonderfully enigmatic piece based on a Breughel painting. In order to transmute it on its way to paperback, my first solution was to place pancakes on the cover.

When we called the author to inform him that we had an idea for the new cover, he said, "Don't tell me: pancakes." So it was back to the drawing board. I attempted a design that had two guys wrestling on the cover.

ABOVE:
Original hardcover design.

RIGHT:
Concepts for paperback.

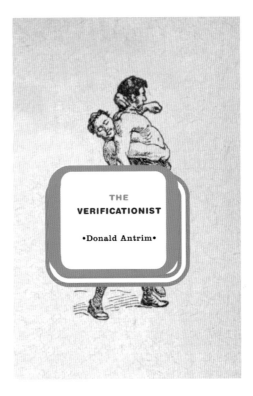

The editor's response was: "Are you sure that these guys, are, um, wrestling?" So next we decided to go with the "crying baby" cover. Perhaps this said more about me than the actual book it was supposed to represent. We followed this with the always-popular vintage road-sign arrows design.

This was trailed by the mysterious floating Wonderbread polka dots. Then the teeny-tiny dog, and the pancake/Breughel compromise special. This prompted another discussion with the author—though for the most part, we bantered about mattresses. Go figure. Finally, ta-dah, the finished product, which makes all the sense in the world once you've read the book.

BELOW:
Further concepts for paperback.

RIGHT:
Final cover.

THE VERIFICATIONIST

Donald Antrim

a novel

"Antrim does a beautiful job . . . [full] of intellection, rude humor, grief and longing."
—*The New York Times Book Review*

BOOK JACKET DESIGN

PROJECT

The Wife

DESIGNER

Barbara DeWilde

CLIENT

Random House

I was commissioned to design a jacket for *The Wife*, a novel by Meg Wolitzer. The story is about a married couple bound together by an enormous secret. He is a famous, philandering novelist on the verge of winning the Nobel Prize; she is a devoted, stay-at-home spouse living in his shadow. Their secret: she has actually authored all of his books.

The simplest step away from a literal design would have been to focus on the fact that this is a book about a relationship and not about writing. Still, I began brainstorming lists of images that related to the text: books, pens, typewriters, ink, paper, words, letters, men of letters, ex libris, ex-spouse, bookplates, monographs, etc. I remembered a book that I was given on ex libris bookplates and I went to look at it. It defined the term as "Ex meaning 'from,' and libris, 'books': an inscription label, or the like, in a book, indicating ownership." The idea of a book and its ownership was such a big theme in this novel that I decided to design a bookplate for the wife character. I limited my design elements to letterforms and that was my way of working for a while. I would only resort to an image if I really needed it. So, I took a W and put it in a box and looked at it. The W needed to have a relationship with something, but I didn't want to use an H.

ABOVE:
Inspiration: an ex libris bookplate.

RIGHT:
Initial sketches.

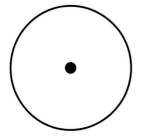

Text and image

I was taught a great lesson on how design is most successful when there is a wide dynamic between the text and the image. My professor, Lanny Sommese, drew a dot on the blackboard and then surrounded the dot with a circle. We were to shout out ideas of what this could represent—an eye, a woman's breast, a wheel—until we were really stretching the relationship between the symbol and its meaning with ideas like fencing foil and the Hindenburg. It took both imagination and audience participation to join the two ideas, which created excitement and interest— something I try to add to everything I work on.

It would look like the Periodic Table. However, the idea of a shadow or another W seemed OK and I started to move them around in relationship to each other. When I flipped the second W upside down, obviously it became an M, and I knew I was onto something: W (women) and M (men), the same and different in relationship to each other. Great. They were also the first and last letters of the author's name, Meg Wolitzer. Kismet!

This is about the point in a design when I start working on my computer. I set up the letterforms using a slim slab serif so that I could use an upside-down W to make an M without it looking funny. I wanted to put something book-like between them, so I made an open-looking book using a bracket from another typeface (still all type—good). The bracket also suggested a mustache on a man. The bookplate was done. Type placement is often suggested by the image and in this case it had to be between them, so it would not get lost. Color choice and border were to stage the other elements. At this point, the fact that this was a design for a bookplate wasn't important, it was just the narrative to get the design dialogue started.

Much of my work is split between magazine design and book jacket design, which are very different areas of publishing. It would be an oversimplification to say that I have a single process for designing, but if pressed I would label my process as "storytelling." This approach for magazine work literally translates into creating a narrative with a beginning, middle, and end. The type needs to be arranged into hierarchies so it can be read in a meaningful sequence, and the story imagery needs to have charm and drama. Much of the design process is about "moving it around"—scaling, juxtaposing, and sequencing the art for maximum impact. For book jackets, the storytelling often involves creating a parallel world to the book, a way to suggest the book's content. I think the word "suggest" is apt since it's only a hint at the depth of the work, hopefully enough to make a reader want to go further and find out more. I also think my most successful work is more of a suggestion of the writing then anything that literally grows out of the story.

RIGHT:
Final cover.

The Essential Principles of Graphic Design

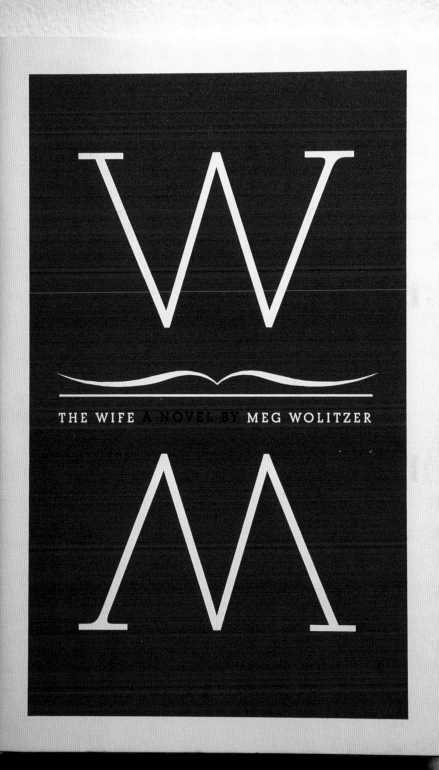

THE WIFE A NOVEL BY MEG WOLITZER

PROJECT

TypeCon 2007

DESIGNER

Marian Bantjes

CLIENT

Society of Typographic Aficionados (SoTA)

I am first and foremost a visual designer. My work may often contain conceptual elements, but this is not where I begin. Usually, I have a fairly immediate vision of what I want the piece to be like. The final piece may not correspond to my original visualization, but this is part of the birth pangs of the process. I do not create exploratory sketches; I do not dabble; I know exactly what I want. The primary challenge involves the struggle in making the imaginary into something concrete.

The beginning is often very simple for me. I sketch with a pencil, and, depending on what I scan into the computer, Photoshop it. Soon after it is printed, I will redraw it by hand until it is exactly how I want it. If the final sketch is to be in vector art, I scan it and trace it by hand in Illustrator—I never use live trace or any other autotracing software. Finally, I make very careful adjustments,

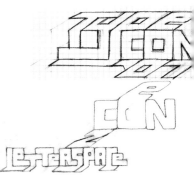

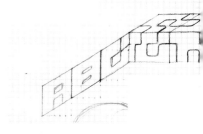

ABOVE:
Initial sketches.

RIGHT:
First direction for exhibit poster.

so that all the curves are perfect. The end result is usually very close to the sketch, only far cleaner, and sometimes more detailed.

Far too often I am forced to scrap what I'm doing and start over. This is the difficult part of the process—letting go. But it's pivotal to do this, for I've come to the conclusion that I'm much better in round one than I am in round two. Needless to say, I could never subscribe to the Beat notion of spontaneous creation. I am, however, still learning the art of giving up, especially when I've invested a lot of time and energy in an idea.

When I'm working with text, I make it as difficult and challenging for myself as possible. I've spent 20 years creating beautifully set type. Now, if I'm not experiencing immense discomfort during the process, I don't think I'm trying hard enough. This has nothing to do with the client, or the project itself. It is about my relationship to design, and my ambition to grow as a typographer.

The Society of Typographic Aficionados (SoTA) commissioned me to create the materials for TypeCon 2007—pro bono. This included the logo, the brochure, and all collateral materials for the organization's annual typography conference. Utterly inspired, I arrived at the conclusion that I wanted to do something with letterforms in isometric space. When they told me their theme for the conference was Letter Space, I couldn't believe my luck!

I wanted to create all sorts of isometric shelves and ledges on which the typography would sit. I'd also planned on using as many three-dimensional fonts as I could get hands on, regardless of perspective or angles. Naturally, this would have made a terrible mess, but I was challenged by the idea and determined to make it work.

To my chagrin, the folks at SoTA were shocked. They were hoping for material similar to that I had created throughout my career. Now, I view these kinds of pro bono jobs as being opportunities to stretch my legs and run the distance, breaking new ground along the way. But we'd reached the point where I had to decide whether I was going to be a prima donna and bolt, or compromise. It is a choice all young graphic designers will have to face at some point in their careers. And, fortunately for all involved, this time I decided to compromise.

The second concept I'd summoned up was nearly identical to the first, only I introduced some of my signature swirls and curves, combined with hand-drawn three-dimensional type. The complex design was so dissimilar to any identity I had come across that I began referring to it as "The Thing." The people at SoTA loved it, and my phrase "All hail The Thing!" became a sort of running joke as we developed the project.

After drawing The Thing in Illustrator, I turned my attention to the poster and program. I had chosen Xavier Dupré's Sanuk as the text face for the materials, so I made three-dimensional versions—based on my isometrics—in three distinct levels: deep letters, not-so-deep letters, and incised letters. The cool thing about isometrics is that it's not true perspective. Objects do not get smaller as they recede into the distance. It's all about lines and placement. These elements were put together in Illustrator, so using them involved placing each letter manually. It was deeply physical work—very much like setting metal type.

I liked to think of The Thing as this gargantuan pile of iron and concrete, like a site-specific installation. It was no longer just a graphic to me. As it existed in space, I was determined that it would continue to exist alone, though it would have to have a landscape to accompany it. At this point it became daunting. Normally, a designer would have supplied The Thing with text guidelines, and enlisted SoTA's aid in completing the program. But I was adamant that the piece I was designing would bring it all together, so I built landscapes and furniture for the

And then for a text face possibly **FF Sanuk** or **Fishmonger** from Suitcase

This might be a Subhead in Sanuk
THIS MIGHT BE A SUB-SUBHEAD: in Sanuk

There will be small bodies of text that wrap and have descriptions of people who are speaking at the conference because they are *very important* and fascinating and we want to know all about them so that we can decide if we want to come to the conference and have piles of fun.

There will be sm wrap and have d are speaking at t they are very imp and we want to that we can deci to the conferenc

FUN @ 6:00pm–11:30pm
All fun comes at a cost of $7.95
See you there.

ABOVE:
Type exploration.

RIGHT:
Exhibition poster.

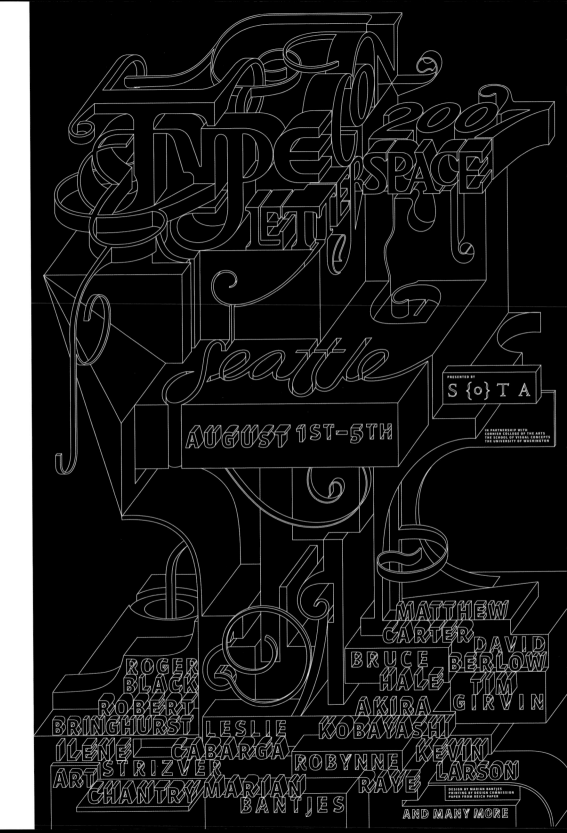

100-plus pages comprising the program brochure. I produced a piece of furniture for each of the 88 designer biographies—all modeled on the same basic shape—and I devised a simple system for the longer, descriptive text passages, that I could adjust by utilizing InDesign. I then introduced fancy custom landscapes that would be located at the forefront of the brochure.

I'm often asked to create pieces that bear close relation to my past work, and I never hesitate to reject projects that outright reflect what has been done previously. As far as I'm concerned, it's up to me to take the risk, and this in turn will show the client how to leap. My very best work comes from the open brief, and I am sympathetic to the fact that such a brief is a very scary place for a client to be, so I applaud their bravery when they agree to move forward.

When I first started out in my own design studio, I made a million mistakes. I didn't properly deal with clients, printers, staff, and, worst of all, my business partner. Most of my mistakes stemmed from the concept of working for money. Naturally, I earn an income now, and I still can't afford to be picky. But to satisfy something deep within me, I really need to be interested in a project, to have a glimpse of some future potential beyond the client's expectations. What I require most of all is a work of absolute complexity, so that I can experience the joy of problem-solving.

Of course, I am frequently lured into taking a job for a check. This is where the decision-making process first kicks in: food, or art, for consumption? It's very difficult to risk financial instability in order to appease the problem-solving demon within me who seeks more complex equations, more abstractions. I've been fortunate in that the risks I have taken have paid off in the past—emotionally, creatively, and financially—but it's a critical, and cringe-inducing, decision to make every single time.

ABOVE:
Cover of exhibition catalog.

RIGHT:
Catalog spread.

PROGRAM DETAILS

TUESDAY JUL 31

MATH FONTS AND THE MICROSOFT MATH ENGINE
10:00AM–1:00PM   Location: **Microsoft Campus**
Presented by **Murray Sargent** and **Sergey Malkin**, Microsoft

Office 2007 comes with a new Math composition engine and the award-winning Cambria Math font. The Microsoft team responsible for math support in Office will describe how the engine works, what it's capable of, and how to make fonts that take advantage of the technology.

WEDNESDAY AUG 1

EXPERT TYPOGRAPHY AND INDESIGN SECRETS
9:00AM–5:30PM   Location: **Cornish College of the Arts**
Presented by **Eric Menninga, Nat McCully,** and
Thomas Phinney, Adobe, **John D. Berry,** and **Jorge de Buen**

This workshop will change your life! A handpicked group of typographic gurus share their best practices and essential tips and tricks. Learn how to make the most of InDesign CS3, from time-saving production techniques and aesthetics to advanced applications like multilingual typesetting. Our experts will also offer in-depth knowledge about how InDesign works and makes decisions so you can make it work better for you.

TOPICS INCLUDE

Computer Typography: *How to Codify Aesthetics*
Good lines vs. bad lines, single-line vs. paragraph line-breaking
Production Features: *Reducing Manual Formatting*
Anchored objects, nested styles, spine-based alignments, OpenType features
Special Topics: *Global Publishing with InDesign CS3*
Greek, Turkish, Vietnamese, Thai, ME languages, Tasmeem
There will be time devoted to Q&A throughout the day to address attendees' unique concerns and workflow.

BEGINNING FONT DESIGN, PART I
9:00AM–12:30PM   Location: **Cornish College of the Arts**
Presented by **Jimmy Gallagher**, FontLab

This is not an advanced class. All material has been designed for beginners.
Students will be introduced to the legacy of extant font families and how they continue to drive modern design. As we cover the basic components and vocabulary, we will design a font together, step by step. The process will include planning the right font for the right project, font formats, how to tackle the positioning and metrics of a font, importing artwork, and understanding vector outlines.
Students will use this knowledge to create test fonts using Fontographer and TypeTool.

FONT QA THE MICROSOFT WAY
9:00AM–12:30PM   Location: **Cornish College of the Arts**
Presented by **Judy Safran-Aasen, Ali Basit**, and **Carolyn Parsons**, Microsoft

Within Microsoft's typography group, you'll hear a familiar mantra: "No product ships without fonts." But the process of taking a request from a product group like Xbox, Zune, Office, or Windows and providing a high-quality tested font is not always straightforward.
In this workshop, the Microsoft typography program management team will walk through the process of scoping, testing, and delivering fonts to the highest level of quality. The Microsoft QA (quality assurance) program will be detailed, from "eyeballing" to "automation." The team will discuss the different approaches taken in updating existing fonts and creating new fonts for various technologies. In addition, they'll detail the process of creating the installation packages (both system-wide and private) they hand off to Microsoft product groups. To round off the session, the team invites you, the TypeCon attendee, to bring your own font, which will be tested and packaged live, before your very eyes.

WORD AS IMAGE: A TYPOGRAPHIC CHARRETTE IN TWO PARTS (1)
9:00AM–12:30PM   Location: **School of Visual Concepts**
Presented by **Jessica Spring**, Springtide Press, and **Jenny Wilkson**, School of Visual Concepts

Drawing from an eclectic collection of lead and wood type and ornaments, participants will collaboratively design and print posters with the help of two experienced guides: Jenny Wilkson, SVC's letterpress shop manager, and Jessica Spring of Springtide Press in Tacoma. The focus will be on achieving top-notch printing on the school's three Vandercook cylinder presses, with a few tricky techniques thrown in along the way.
In addition to their own personal work, the morning session's participants will also produce several partially printed designs for the afternoon session to complete in their unique way. The guaranteed-to-be-stunning suite of prints from this inaugural TypeCon collaboration will be displayed Thursday-Sunday at the Crowne Plaza, and proceeds from their sale will benefit SOTA's Education Fund.
This workshop is open to attendees at all levels of experience. What's a charrette? en.wikipedia.org/wiki/Charrette

PROJECT

McSweeney's Issue 23

DESIGNER

Andrea Deszö

CLIENT

McSweeney's

My projects begin the moment my eyes open up to the pillow or ceiling, in the bathtub and kitchen, halls and stairs, the long sidewalks, and chattering subways. I'm fond of the anonymity of those places, the fact that there is no performance anxiety because I am alone with myself. Once an idea pops into my head, I have to scramble to my notebook and sketch it in before it fades away into oblivion. Sometimes I get a very clear vision of what the piece will look like. Other times it is wavy and washed-over, as if I'm looking at something from a distance. When I sketch, I use a thick, blunt color pencil. Once I begin to see the image clearer in my mind, I begin using sharper pencils—the sharpening vision corresponds to the sharpness of the pencils' tips.

The next step depends on the techniques I wish to use: drawing, painting, sculpture, embroidery, paper cuts, and shadow puppets—whatever is best to express my vision. I created *Lessons From My Mother*, a series of 50 narrative embroideries with Transylvanian superstitions as its subject, mainly on the subway and while waiting in line at the supermarket or bank.

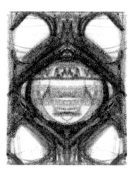

ABOVE:
Initial sketch.

RIGHT:
Sketch redrawn.

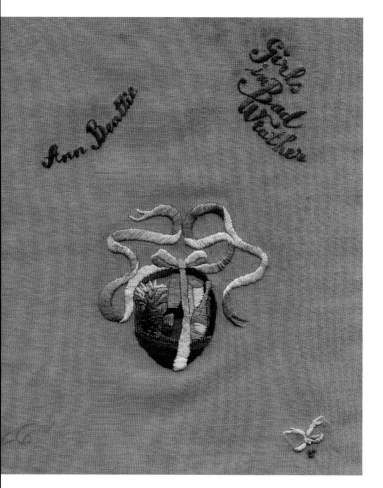

I work with computers for "production" purposes. It helps save time on resizing, pattern repetition, and color alterations. Using a computer never influences how my pieces work or look, but I try to keep its use to a minimum. I was commissioned to do a project for the 23rd issue of a quarterly literary magazine titled *McSweeney's*. The work comprised 10 individual front and back covers—one for each story in the publication and one that folded out into a poster. The project was commissioned by *McSweeney's* managing editor, Eli Horowitz, an inspiring man who always made himself available as a springboard and gentle coaxer throughout the three weeks it took to bring the piece into fruition. I honestly could not have done it without him.

I decided to create a large mirrored pattern, posing as a book jacket, with various sections that could be used as one-of-a-kind frames on individual covers. The sections were all cut from a different area of the pattern itself, so even though each appeared distinct, they still could be recognized as part of the same family. I drew a quarter of the pattern in black and white pencil, mirrored it, and began assembling within the computer. I used the blank spaces in the pattern as windows, which served two purposes. Through each window the reader could not only spy on the particular world of each and every story, but also see the authors and titles that were the founding inspiration.

The uniqueness of each author's voice was conveyed using a wide variety of techniques, such as creating collages and articulating shadow puppets, and all the written titles were hand-painted. I loved working on this project, even though I only slept three hours a night for two weeks straight.

LEFT:
Original embroidery, paintings, shadow puppets, and paper cuts.

FOLLOWING PAGES:
Sketches and concepts, including working notes on the colors used.

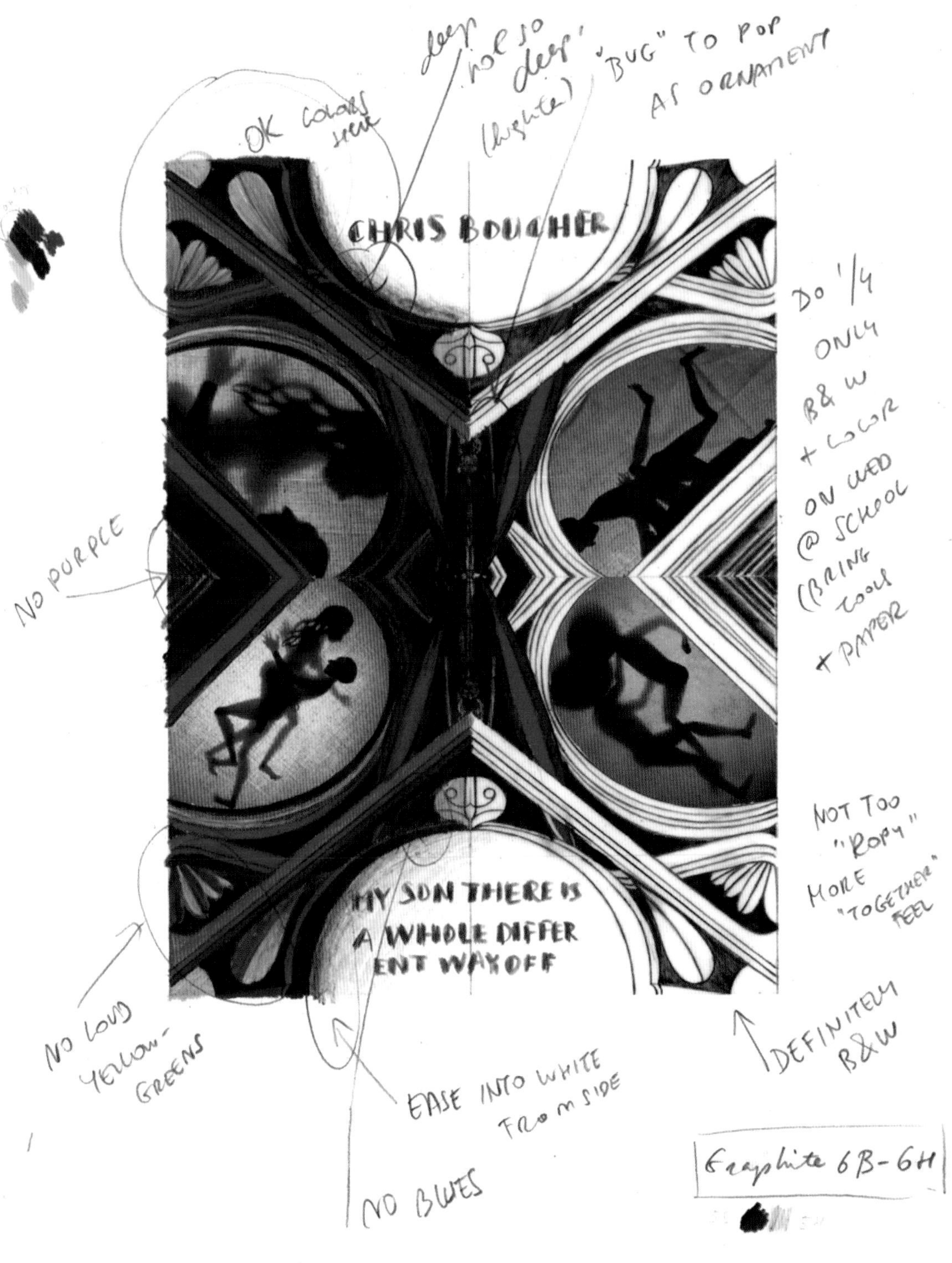

deep "not so deep" (lighter) "BUG" TO POP AS ORNAMENT

OK COLORS HERE

CHRIS BOUCHER

DO 1/4 ONLY B&W + COLOR ON WED @ SCHOOL (BRING TOOLS + PAPER

NO PURPLE

MY SON THERE IS A WHOLE DIFFER ENT WAY OFF

NOT TOO "ROPY" MORE "TOGETHER" FEEL

NO LOUD YELLOW-GREENS

EASE INTO WHITE FROM SIDE

DEFINITELY B&W

NO BLUES

Graphite 6B-6H

The Man Who Ate Michael Rockefeller

THE MAN WHO ATE MICHAEL ROCKEFELLER

The Man Who Ate Michael Rockefeller

Christopher Stokes

The Man Who Ate Michael Rockefeller

Christopher Stokes

The Man Who Ate Michael Rockefeller

Christopher Stokes

THE MAN WHO ATE MICHAEL ROCKEFELLER

The Man Who Ate Michael Rockefeller

CAREN BEILIN
I'M THE BOSS
SO DO
WHAT I SAY

BLACK HOODIE

Clancy Martin

How To Sell

LEFT:
Final cover.

RIGHT:
Final cover, unfolded.

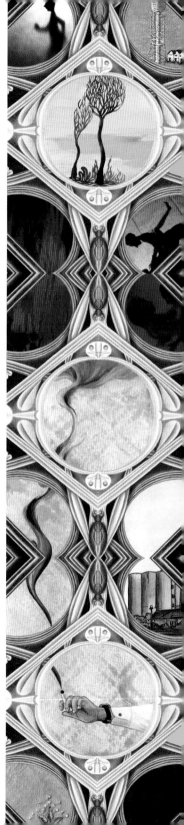

STORIES BY

Chris Bachelder,
Ann Beattie, Caron Beilin,
Roddy Doyle, Clancy Martin,
Deb Olin Unferth, Chris Stokes,
Wells Tower, Shawn Vestal,
April Wilder.

ART BY ANDREA DEZSÖ

McSweeney's 23

PROJECT

365: AIGA Year In Design 28

DESIGNER

Rick Valicenti, Thirst

CLIENT

AIGA, The Professional Association for Design

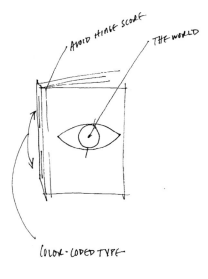

Each year, the American Institute of Graphic Arts (AIGA) holds two prestigious competitions that recognize the best work in the industry. The 365: Annual Design Competition showcases cross-sections of design, from branding to packaging to interactive experience design. The 50 Books/50 Covers Competition showcases works from the world of publishing.

The competition annual is divided into a subjective cover, overture, and section divider reviewing the year of 2006 at a glance and an objective portfolio section presenting all of the competition winners with respect and equality. Both sections were conceived and designed independent of one another in order to ensure contrast.

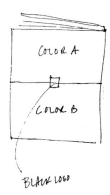

Subjective Cover

The work in this book represented the world in 2006, as seen through the eyes of the American design community.

Subjective Overture

Collages of pictures donated from Getty Images are positioned on the globe to represent a specific country or region. In total, 1,580 images from four different regions (the USA, China, South America, and Africa) were used. Two photographs are consciously enlarged. Through juxtaposition they create a tongue-in-cheek statement about the culture du jour.

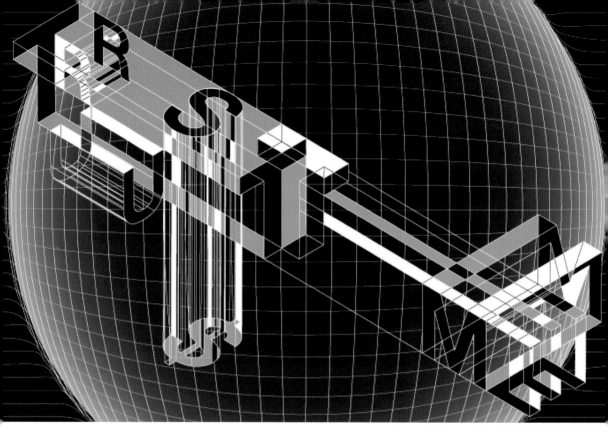

Subjective section dividers

Explosive typography underscores the message, expressing a very self-centered interpretation of each design category:

FEEL ME: EXPERIENCE DESIGN

BELIEVE ME: INFORMATION DESIGN

ME ME ME: PROMOTIONAL DESIGN

CONSU ME: PACKAGE DESIGN

TRU$T ME: CORPORATE COMMUNICATIONS

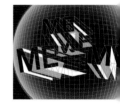

ABOVE:
Subjective section dividers.

Objective portfolio

The work of the competition winners is presented within a neutral grid structure, maintaining a "white gallery" background, showcasing the work in a respectful manner.

The grid is fiercely disciplined, with the work on the left-hand side scaling up to a predetermined width from the lower-left corner of the spread, and the right-hand work scaling down from the upper-right corner. Full-spread images begin in the lower-right corner, flush to the right margin, and extend in width across the spread.

Captions retain a level of typographic detail, separating the information in a unique manner. Only the core information is presented, bestowing as much respect for the imagery as possible.

Custom automation programming, written by Thirst, allowed the design of the entire 250-page section to be typeset and placed in just under 60 minutes. The InDesign software automatically plotted all the captions and imagery from the database.

BELOW:
Interior spreads featuring the custom automation programming written by Thirst.

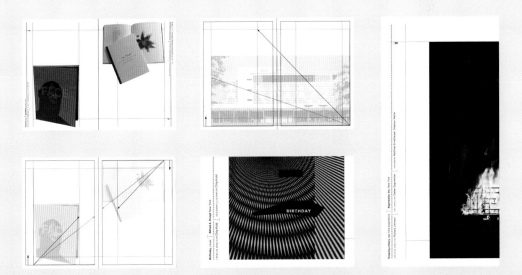

PROJECT

Dinero Covers

DESIGNER

Patrick Thomas

CLIENT

Dinero, The Financial Supplement to *La Vanguardia*

I approach each client and project differently. There is no house style within the studio that I am aware of. We have a large library of reference materials and I keep numerous notebooks, which I use to feed my own work. If I have a mental block, I browse through these materials to kickstart the creative process.

In Spain, I am best known for my collaboration with the financial supplement of La Vanguardia, titled Dinero, for which I've illustrated in excess of 150 covers. Ironically, they rejected my first cover. My proposal didn't fit the style of illustration they were considering at the time, but gradually they came around to my way of thinking and, to their credit, gave me incommensurable freedom. In this way, each project was forced to adapt to me. Moving from London to Barcelona 16 years ago could have been professional suicide—huge drop in design fees, lower standard of work, etc.

ABOVE:
Rejected cover.

RIGHT:
Art Falsification cover.

FOLLOWING PAGES:
Petroleum cover.

Africa cover.

DINERO

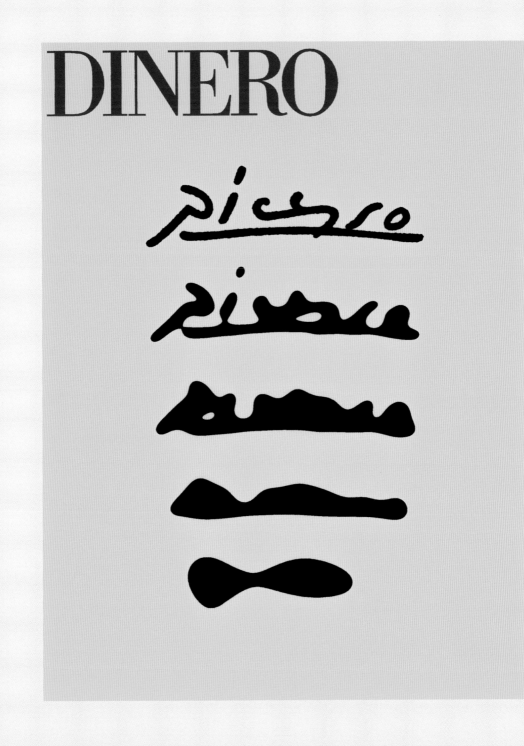

DINERO

DINERO

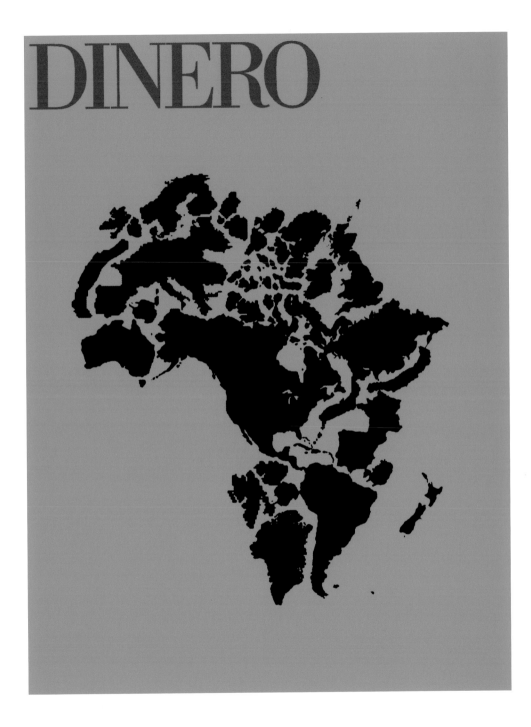

DINERO

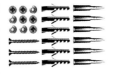

DINERO

ABOVE:
Rebuilding Iraq cover.

LEFT:
American Investment in Cuba cover.

But in retrospect, looking at my clients and my quality of life, I consider it a lucky choice. The work I do for the press tends to be the worst paid and the most stressful. Since these stints constitute a small part of my professional output, I have to juggle several jobs at once. There is a certain danger in repeating myself, and the challenge lies in the ways I can manage to convey a measure of surprise. Most covers are commissioned 24 hours before they go to print, and on quite a few occasions I've only had a few hours to work. Though the printing and paper is often of poor quality, and the work has a lifespan of only a few seconds, it is without a doubt the most satisfying work I do. I regard it as a fantastic opportunity to communicate with the public directly—it's like I'm eating a forkful of eggs right beside them at their breakfast tables.

"American Investment in Cuba" began as a list of American multinational corporations published by *Fortune 500*. I picked the top 20 and played around with them. I enjoy using clichés and appropriating existing images, so the logical route seemed to be the most obvious way to go. The challenge was to make an iconic image mine. The idea of making a monumental image out of smaller components appealed to me.

While I was working on the cover for "Rebuilding Iraq," I was, auspiciously it would turn out, reconstructing my studio. The building materials lying all about me burned a concise image into my mind, and that's how I came to use *objets trouvés* in this particular work.

I receive briefs during telephone conferences, so I always have a pencil handy in order to jot down key themes and doodle ideas. This might sound surprising since there is very little drawing evident in the finished product. I really like the idea of conjuring images without drawing or painting. I'm sure this is a rebellious reaction to the prevalence of the image in our media-saturated age, where anything and everything is available by the click of the mouse and the soundless thrum of working search engines.

MAGAZINE DESIGN

PROJECT

Theme Magazine

DESIGNER

Jiae Kim & John Lee

CLIENT

Theme Magazine

When my husband and partner John H. Lee and I founded *Theme* magazine, we had three months to print the first issue. We committed to the project in September 2004, and by January 2005 our first issue went to press. We defined the look of the magazine, including the logo, in less than a month. At first, we'd leaned toward a neutral typeface for the masthead, something that could be filled in with a new theme each issue. Thankfully, our board of advisers (the legendary art director John C. Jay among them) gave us invaluable critical feedback. Since our lead time was brief, we mocked things up in order to convey an idea without fussing over whether it looked good or not. A lot of the stuff was pretty hideous, though the resulting logo was handsome.

John and I have a great collaborative relationship. We understand how to pursue the creative flow and to keep the current running strong. Instead of rejecting ideas, we usually latch onto some part in order to inspire a newer, stronger one, which leads to further speculation. Of course, sometimes an idea is so awful that we have to stomp on it before it can snowball on us and roll us down the wrong path.

RIGHT:

Initial logo explorations.

The final logo.

Inspiration for the final logo.

theme   :*theme*   **theme:**   THEME

THEME

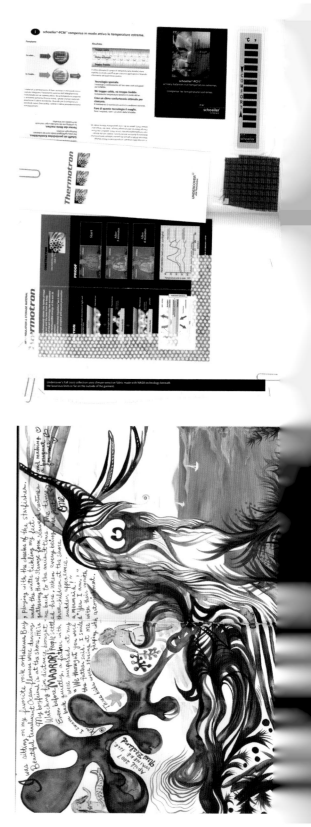

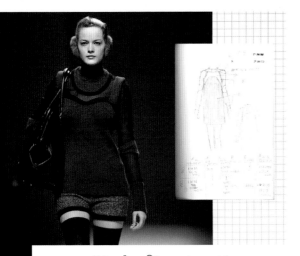

Under Construction

Fashion wunderkind Jun Takahashi reinvents himself.

INTERVIEW BY **MADSAKI** PORTRAIT BY **DEE** TRANSLATION BY **ERI HAMAJI**
IMAGES COURTESY OF **UNDERCOVER**

left: Fall 2007 runway photo
right: Jun Takahashi's Fall 2007 collection sketch

After an idea is fully formed, we play "design ping pong." Sometimes I'll start the design; other times John will. But it always bounces from one to the other until both of us agree that it works. It helps that we have similar aesthetics and guidelines—we're not flashy, and substance is always critical. The positive side of being both client and designer is that we get to articulate what we need as we're designing, which is convenient.

Design is simply about communicating, and the tools at hand are typography, color, and composition. It's beneficial to your craft to have something interesting to say, and if you've mastered all the tools, then the resulting construction will be interesting as well as sound. What I love most about editorial design is that you literally say something, and then drive it home with the force of your design.

When we make mistakes, it is usually because we didn't trust our instincts, and we didn't take the time to really work out the design. As we generally have two weeks to design each issue of the magazine, one of these mistakes always lies in wait. The upside is that we get to correct the mistakes we've made from issue to issue, learning as we proceed.

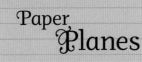

Paper Planes

The Travel Journals of Barnstormer Yuri Shimojo

INTERVIEW BY **JOHN LEE** PORTRAIT BY **GION**
IMAGES COURTESY OF **YURI SHIMOJO AND CWC INTERNATIONAL**

These days everyone's got a blog, but the problem with blogs is they're not very colorful. Sure, you can add fancy flash animation, brightly-hued jpegs from the latest digicam, or kinetically expressive .mov files, but the tactility disappears; web journals simply don't compare to a beautifully illustrated, handwritten notebook.

No one understands this better than Yuri Shimojo. The 41-year-old artist, illustrator, author, and Barnstormer lives life to the fullest; and, luckily for us, she documents it in physical journals that are nothing short of brilliant. Whether she's in Brooklyn, Tokyo, or Maui, Shimojo succinctly captures the essence of unusual creatures living next to fantastic people in faraway places.

LEFT:
Covers for *Theme.*

Spreads from *Theme.*

MAGAZINE DESIGN

PROJECT

Orange Life

DESIGNER

Vault49

CLIENT

Orange Life

Following intense brainstorming sessions, long hours of listening, and delving deeply into design briefs, concepts are born. We pride ourselves on our ideas as much as we do our execution and believe that the art of design collaboration, based expressly on cooperation and profound creativity, creates work that is far more than the mere sum of its parts. We also find ourselves bored with our work long before others, so, by risky experimentation, we constantly grow as designers, and develop our toolkits. The concept that "the devil is in the detail" is one we wholly espouse. We believe that our art direction is unique because we successfully fuse the skills of many talented designers, photographers, and illustrators, and we pride ourselves on our hi-tech expertise, which we combine with a natural love for manual production processes.

We recently art-directed a magazine cover for *Orange Life*. We directed the photoshoot and developed the entire design.

RIGHT:
A frame from the initial photo shoot.

Final cover for *Orange Life*.

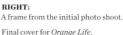

The brief given to us by the client was entitled "What To Wear." We imagined the typical scene of a girl at home on a Saturday evening getting ready for a night out, in love with fashion and surrounded by fine clothing and beautiful accoutrements, yet unable to find the right thing to wear. The nude shoot was the "blank canvas" from which we explored our model's fashion dilemma.

We went through a rigorous process in order to create this piece, which included the following:

- Photographer selection
- Model casting
- Hair and makeup selection
- Development of background textures and the graphic design of all the elements
- The actual photoshoot
- Photography retouching and continued work on illustration elements

PROJECT

SEE: The Potential of Place

DESIGNER

Bill Cahan, Cahan Associates

CLIENT

Herman Miller

SEE: The Potential of Place is a magazine used as a vehicle to reinforce Herman Miller's image as a leading developer and innovative purveyor of information. Its name was developed by Herman Miller—a nod to George Nelson and his classic, influential book, *How To See*.

When we were asked to participate in a design audition for the magazine, we were supplied with the name and text for three sample articles. Our assignment was to design the cover and a couple of sample spreads. We really wanted the job, so we wound up designing six completely different prototypes, from cover to cover. After all, what designer in their right mind would not want to work with Herman Miller?

Herman Miller provided us with the most inspiring and creative brief we'd ever received. It contained words like "spontaneous," "eclectic," and "disruptive." By this personal expression, we knew

RIGHT:
The original brief from Herman Miller, with Bill Cahan's notes.

[handwritten: EXTENSION 26 TH]

March 18, 2004

Bill Cahan
Cahan Associates
171 Second Street
San Francisco, CA 94105

[handwritten: SEEING IN A NEW WAY]

[handwritten: WORKPLACE ALLSPACE STEELCASE NEOCON]

Hi, Bill

Thanks for your interest in this project.

Through this "audition" we plan to identify the resource most appropriate to produce, with us, the first issue of a periodic publication, *SEE: The Potential of Your Space*. It will showcase Herman Miller's knowledge and reinforce our position as an expert in Great Places. The audiences for this publication are primarily customers, including facility managers, corporate decision makers, and A&D; secondarily, we'll reach Herman Miller's own employees, salespeople, and dealers. We'd like to publish the first issue of this publication to coincide with our company's major sales event, which occurs in late September.

[handwritten: Place]

Our objectives for the publication are these:
•   Create and/or reinforce Herman Miller's image as a developer and purveyor of information that's valuable to the creation of Great Places.
•   Provide the opportunity to showcase new Herman Miller knowledge as it's developed.
•   Support substantive diagnostic discussions with customers regarding their current issues.
•   Support salespeople and others (e.g., dealer marketers, A&D reps) in making non-project contact with customers or prospective customers, building or maintaining relationships.

We envision the publication as
•   unpredictable
•   inconsistent
•   eclectic
•   disruptive
•   a spontaneous creation
•   a personal expression
•   consistent with Herman Miller's brand dimensions (spirited, purposeful, and human)

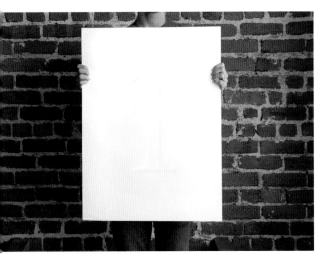

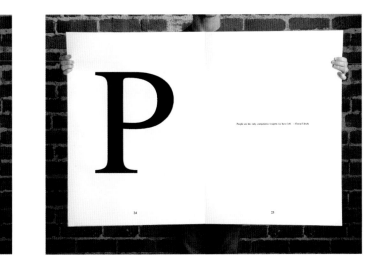

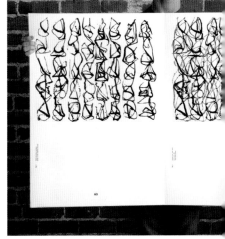

that they were expecting something no one had ever seen before. By the same token, they wanted the magazine to continue to align with their brand dimensions: spirited, purposeful, human. The magazine was and is driven by the heavy content geared to the architectural and design community. It would have been too simple to reference visuals of buildings and places in a literal way; our approach relied on giving each article its own flavor.

Our team was comprised of editors, writers, art directors, designers, photographers, illustrators, and production managers, all working together seamlessly in glorious harmony. The photographers and illustrators were often culled from a global pool, and the criteria were always based upon who we thought would be able to bring the most out of the chosen concept. The talent we hired often brought their own interpretation to the stories we wished to tell, so there really wasn't a creative style we adhered to religiously.

The making of each issue of the magazine always required one month of research, one month of design execution, and one month of product development. We leaned heavily on metaphor and idea, concepts that were not immediately obvious, granting the magazine an artful yet intellectual air. At first glance, *SEE* can feel intimidating, but the more time one is willing to spend wallowing in the content, the clearer the relationship becomes between the words and the visuals. Every turn of the page was a building-up of concepts, cinematic in pacing and storytelling. Our ultimate goal was to create a magazine that would pull and delight the reader in new and unexpected ways. And what resulted was a particular style: simple, clean yet understated, punctuated with bold and captivating visuals.

The design of the selected prototype remained intact when we used it in the premier issue. Many of the articles were only slightly modified, in order to accommodate the change in content. What did change, however, was the cover: the "See" pattern within the masthead was intended to blind emboss. The magazine's underlying grid was permeable, so that the reader could deconstruct the magazine if they felt so inclined. Each issue was very image-intensive, almost cinematic, and we wanted people to be able to pull the issue apart if they wanted to save any portions, or wallpaper their rooms with any of their personal favorites.

ABOVE:
First cover of *SEE*.

RIGHT:
Spreads from the first issue of *SEE*.

The prototype's color pattern did not make it into the final design. The colors we did use were developed from Herman Miller product finishes and fabric swatches—a nod to fabric designer Alexander Girard. Each one of the hundreds of colors was shown with its respective swatch name and number. As the design of the interior developed—and because there wasn't any advertising—we realized that there was a need to signal where one article finished and the next began. This is why we introduced the colors, which would become *SEE*'s signature.

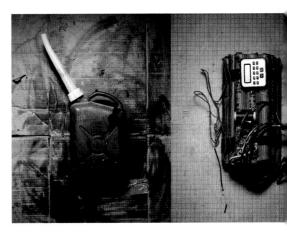

POSTER DESIGN

PROJECT

The Taming of the Shrew

DESIGNER

Luba Lukova

CLIENT

Columbia University

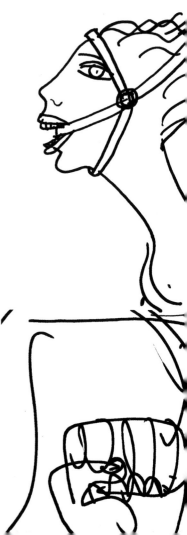

I always begin a project with research, to learn as much as possible about my subject. I study photographs and images related to the themes at hand, attend rehearsals, and participate in discussions with theater directors and editors. I carefully read the books, plays, or articles I am going to create designs for. Only then do I begin my sketches. The more experienced I become, the less I have to commit to paper in order to find an idea that will work.

The poster I designed for Columbia University's production of *The Taming of the Shrew* involved at least 50 sketches. This may seem grueling, but I truly enjoyed the process. Shakespeare's play is so well known that the real challenge was coming up with an original concept. The Columbia production was a modern interpretation, and it struck me as old-fashioned to explore the idea of "taming a woman." What I was searching for was an image that would represent the relationship between the two main characters, Katherine and Petruccio, in order to make them inter-dependent. Yet another possibility was to find a metaphor for Katherine's transformation from "shrew" to "submissive wife."

At first, my client decided to go with the image of a bra composed of two female faces. I found this to be surprising and humorous, for not only was it representative of comedy, it also spoke of rebellion, particularly that era in which women burned their bras. After a second discussion with the director, we decided to go with the image of a muzzle. This was not a tacky rendering of the battle of the sexes. Instead, it suggested that we as a human race need to temper our anger in order to survive in society.

The important thing to remember is that good design is universal. It spans continents and touches the high as well as the low. As long as the work is moving, people's reactions will be of a kind, no matter whether they lives in a ghetto or a gated community. Human beings have profound emotions, and graphic designers have the ability to touch the necessary chords.

PREVIOUS PAGES:
Initial sketches for poster.

BELOW:
First direction for poster.

RIGHT:
Final poster.

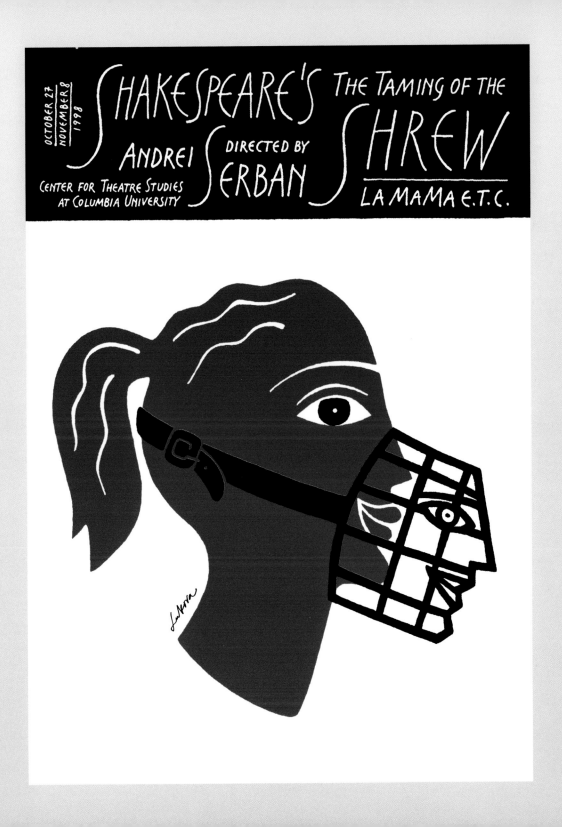

Annual Economics Issue

Christoph Niemann

The New York Times Magazine

I rarely do research for a new project. When I work for "general audience" publications, it is important that my readers understand what I have drawn, even before they read the article. I try to stay on top of current events, so the illustrations are created in context from the start. I'm only given a few hours a day to come up with a concept, so I'd be in big trouble if I first had to learn what filibusters, green zones, and sub-prime mortgages were. As my terrific professor, Heinz Edelmann, often told us: "You will be surprised how many problems can be solved through hard work."

I always try to make every single illustration the funniest, smartest, cutest, smuggest, and most perfectly rendered piece of work in existence, which is not always the best idea. Different work requires different measures. To throw in a cooking metaphor: I had the habit of tossing food into my big steel pan and cranking up the flames to 600 degrees, because I wanted that meal to sizzle and hiss, to throw smoke and spit fire. It was only after I'd worked as an art director

RIGHT:
First sketch for the "Debt" cover.

that I began to appreciate new methods in the craft of cookery. For one thing, some dishes were best prepared lukewarm.

For the cover of The *New York Times Magazine*, Rem Duplessis, the art director for the magazine, called me to work on the cover for the annual economics issue. The topic was the crushing debt, via credit cards and mortgage loans, that threatened the stability of the economy. Debt is one of those topics that happen to be great for an illustration, since it cannot be summoned visually without an accompanying picture. We thought it would be fun to transform the letters D, E, B, T into a gigantic evil monster, threatening to crush anyone in its vicinity. Once we had the idea, what followed was primarily a graphic exercise: I attempted the creation of a single monster with all four letters, but ultimately we had to settle upon a gang of four furry creatures with flailing arms. Initially, we wanted to display the people in an abstracted way—bodiless heads running away on hands and feet—but after playing around with some versions we realized that the imagery would work better if the monster were contrasted with a realistic crowd of people. This final vision gave the reader a better angle, allowing them to identify with those suffering with weighty debt.

ABOVE:
Later sketches.

RIGHT:
Final cover: "America's Scariest Addiction Is Getting Even Scarier."

The Money Issue

The New York Times Magazine

JUNE 11, 2006 / SECTION 6

DEBT

America's Scariest
Addiction Is Getting Even Scarier

NIALL FERGUSON: WHAT UNDOES A SUPERPOWER MOST JON GERTNER: RETABULATING STUDENT LOANS JACKSON LEARS: HOW WE MORALIZE.
AND DON'T, ABOUT BORROWING SPIKE GILLESPIE: BANKRUPT AND FREE! ALEX KOTLOWITZ: AN IMMIGRANT'S PRICE FOR COMING HERE MATTATHIAS SCHWARTZ:
TAKEN TO THE BANK BY ONLINE POKER WALTER KIRN: MORTGAGED COMMITMENTS ROB WALKER: CLEANING UP IN PAWNSHOPS AND MORE...

PROJECT

Annual Report 2003-2006

DESIGNER

Richard Colbourne, Addison

CLIENT

iStar Financial

The most significant communication a public company provides to shareholders and the financial community is the annual report. As a result, the first phase in creating one involves the absorption of an enormous amount of information. This is achieved by interviewing key stakeholders concerning the higher objectives of the brand, and results in a deeper understanding of the corporation's issues. Once the facts are acquired, the message emphasis and visual hierarchy must be designated. I always ask my clients to boil the creative brief down to the single most important message, which, though enlightening, often proves difficult. Designers can never assume clients want what they ask for! In the past, this has led me to design projects that were underwhelming or simply wrong. Graphic designers must dazzle the client at every turn and learn to think for themselves. Although a client may be conservative, it is still possible to inspire them. By refusing to lower the bar, you raise the probability of great design.

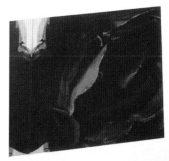

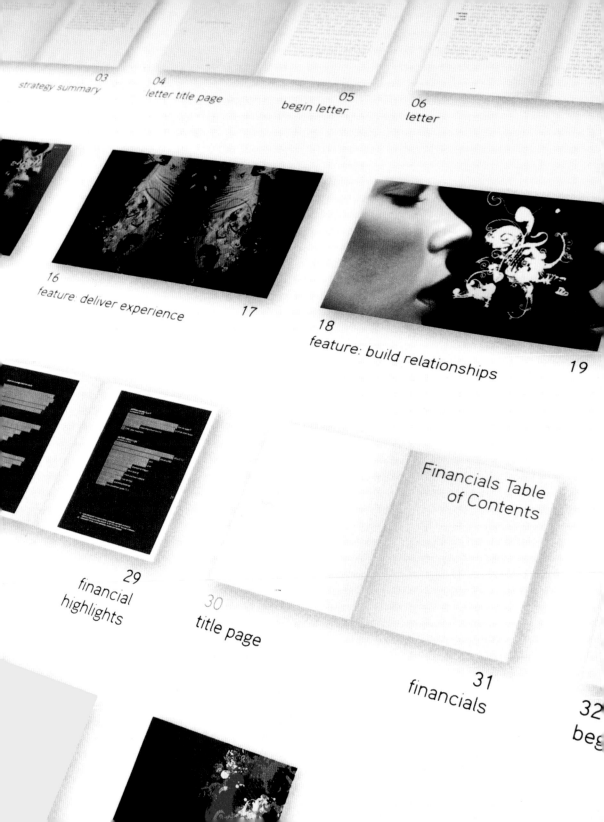

The creative journey in developing an annual report requires trust, which is gained by understanding the corporation's business in depth and exploring ideas with the chief executive officer early in the process. For iStar, this crucial collaboration allowed for a brand transformation that was supported at all levels.

Once we have this information, we present the idea in words, avoiding the distraction of subjective visual elements. There have been numerous instances in which outstanding ideas have been eliminated because a client didn't like sans-serif type or cutting-edge photography. We present three to five message frameworks in the form of thumbnails, resulting in a clear concept direction.

Having defined the strategic approach, design can then drive the message home. For iStar, excellent design execution was driven by the need to position the company as the ultimate choice in its class.

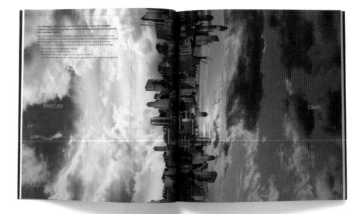

Over the last seven years, our work for iStar has been extremely fulfilling. From a creative perspective, we went beyond the limits of financial literature and advertising. We established a luxury brand where there was none, by introducing the guiding concept of "the ultra"—achieving the highest level of sophistication. Design was the engine that drove the message home. In producing effective communication, strategy can only get you halfway to your destination. Intuition and creative spirit provide the spark. iStar believed that excellent design execution was crucial to its success. The company is now a leader in communication.

The business mind is often a conservative one. Clients want to see precedents in other companies, they desire predictability, and they find it difficult to make giant leaps. However, iStar continues to understand the significant value of innovation and can envision the future potential of unique ideas—something that has been rewarding for the brand and all of its constituents.

LEFT:
2003 annual report for iStar.

2005 annual report for iStar.

2006 annual report for iStar.

BELOW:
Annual report box set. A five-year strategy for iStar Financial was emphasized by delivering a box with the annual report. Space for the next four annual reports shows a commitment to the company strategy.

PROJECT

Corporate Identity

DESIGNER

Connie Birdsall, Lippincott

CLIENT

Delta Airlines

The paradox of design

We live in an oversaturated visual environment. Due to the prevalence of like-minded companies, striving for the same design goals, it becomes more of a challenge to create something truly unique. It is relatively easy to create a new identity, but real change occurs over a long period of time. Implementing the brand across all touch points is difficult for most companies to stomach, for they have a tendency to rely upon their icons to express their story. Though it is true that a strong concept will convey a few aspects of the business, without a voice and visual language to support company goals, as well as a solid pledge of commitment from senior management, the icon will remain flat and unrealized.

Selling design is just as difficult as developing it. It is critical to take great care in creating a slick logic and a hard rationale in order to convince a client of the value of a design's architecture. To do this successfully, one must learn about the client's business, values, aspirations, and communication needs. There must be a long study of the evolution of mergers, acquisitions, and spin-offs. This is hard

work, and should never be boring. If there is a lack of interest in the task, it is wiser to jettison the project before it's too late. Otherwise, the lifespan of the identity you create will be short indeed.

One of the paradoxes of design is that while it is always evolving, it mysteriously remains the same. Though there are alterations within the environment, strong brands and identity hold up to the test of time. Never present anything you consider to be below par, for the designs we put out into the world often have a very long shelf life.

Design solutions

To develop a good solution, it is essential to implement the criteria for guiding the design evolution, as well as the assessment of all creative ideas. The criteria include reviews of the competitive environment, trends, culture, marketplace perceptions, target segment priorities, equity drivers, communication positioning, image attributes, and company structure. This strategy provides an aid in building the brand architecture, and, once that is developed, there is a close examination of where the brand will live in the world—from signage and online applications, to retail environments and co-sponsorship with other brands. This is an exploratory, creative process, which demands a lot of questions in order to find the right answer.

Degrees of Identity Change

Refresh: Graphic change represented in a slightly modified name and/or logo, color, and typography to signal change with continuity.

Evolution: Design change that leverages current or heritage name and/or elements, to signal new positioning strategy.

Revolution: Significant change represented by an entirely new name and/or logo, to signal a break from the past, an entirely new direction.

If an existing identity is already in place, a new set of questions needs to be explored. Are we refreshing the identity to signal change with continuity? Are we looking to express a completely revolutionary design that will trumpet significant change? Do we want to break away from standard industry language and differentiate ourselves? And do we need a standalone symbol?

If a lengthy name is involved, then a standalone symbol can be used as a telegraphic method to communicate the brand, especially if a consumer brand is involved. This means that there is potential to create equity through the brand's expression, as long as the company is willing to spend a significant amount of money on the launching and support of the identity. If the company's name is an acronym, then a symbol is a nifty way to express the key message about the essence of the brand. Yet, if a company already has a longstanding symbol, one that has been used on everything from cufflinks to pins, it would be very difficult to select a design that is comprised of a simple word mark alone.

Design development

Once all the questions are answered, then the foundation is set. We start the process by bringing in a team of three to five designers, together with the lead strategy partner and the design partner, to discuss the creative brief we have developed. The brief articulates the brand strategy, including the positioning, desired image attributes, competitive opportunities, white spaces for color or iconography, and all the pertinent functional criteria. The team brainstorms to determine the many paths that could be taken, and explores the symbol. The designers then work independently, developing visual directions.

The first phase of development involves a broadening of conceptions. Designs are placed on a critiquing wall, and every four days or so we review the progress as a team. Once we're certain that we've gone as far as we can, we begin to narrow our choices, using the criteria as a filter to evaluate each of the design directions. We select five to seven designs for the first round of presentations.

Classic Corporate Identities

Coca-Cola: a ubiquitous global consistency and masterful execution, as well as equity ownership of the color red, aids their reputation as a top-tier company.

Target: a consistent trend-setter unafraid of modern design language. Target helps make good design accessible to the mass market.

Starbucks: a category inventor with its own global design language, which it applies with the right amount of local flexibility and variety. It also capitalizes on a trend that brings the European experience into the US market.

Nike: sets the standard for inspirational positioning and provocative design, both in communicatory ventures and the products themselves.

Apple: contains all of the above, plus an extraordinary visual restraint and discipline. Apple have mastered the art of reinvention and are always brilliantly on-brand.

BELOW:
Broad conceptual exploration for
the Sprint identity.

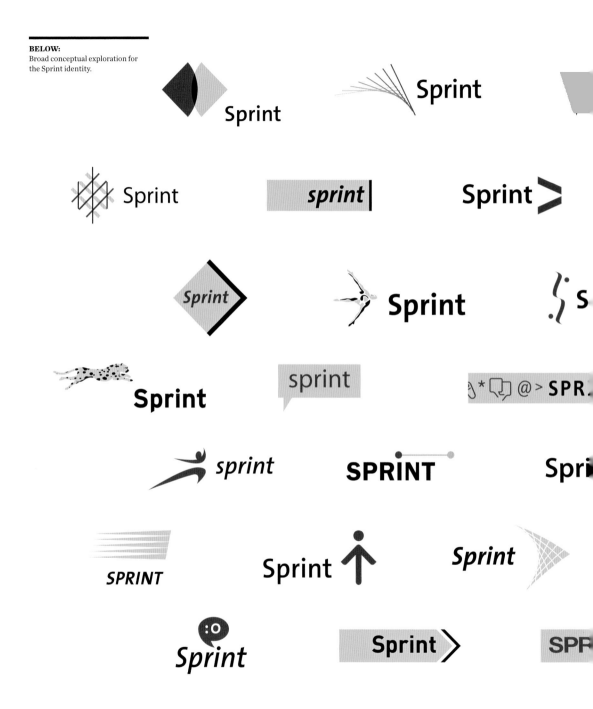

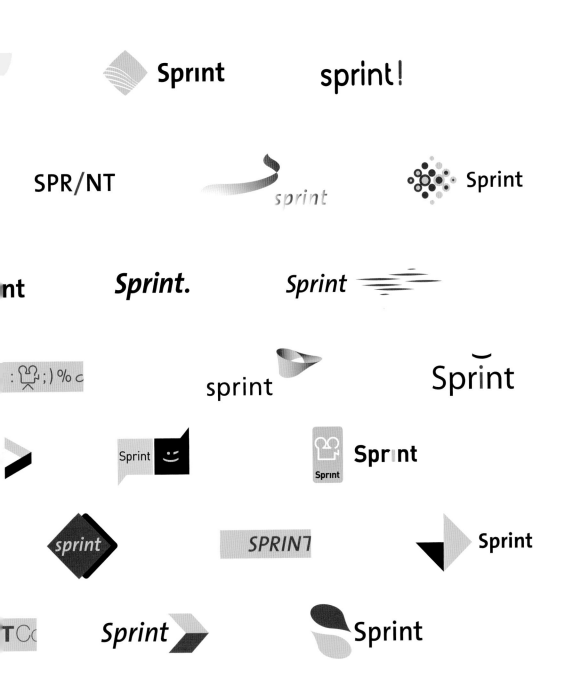

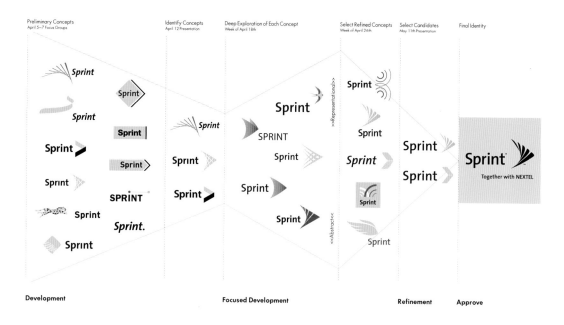

Preliminary Concepts
April 5–7 Focus Groups

Identify Concepts
April 12 Presentation

Deep Exploration of Each Concept
Week of April 18th

Select Refined Concepts
Week of April 26th

Select Candidates
May 11th Presentation

Final Identity

Development

Focused Development

Refinement

Approve

In terms of graphics, we're searching for solutions that embody one simple visual idea in a strong and memorable design. Designs that cram in too many concepts begin to feel like graphic calisthenics—they overwork the minds of the audience, making them much less memorable. As we move toward refinement, we're looking at the craft of the designs and the ideas they convey with equal attention.

The Sprint logo exploration shown here demonstrates a typical progression: broad, then narrow, then broadly casting out once again in order to focus on a few core ideas, and then a narrowing to the final design. It is a very iterative process.

ABOVE:
Stages in the Sprint identity development process.

RIGHT:
New Delta Airlines identity.

Delta Airlines

Recently, we worked with Delta Airlines, where the average employee tenure is 25 years—loyalty is a surplus here. The Delta symbol, affectionately called "the widget" by employees, was so highly revered that the management team suggested that it should not be touched. We were told horror stories about one of the recent design variations. Employees set off on a witch-hunt, eager to burn what was dubbed the "frowny face" widget at the stake. The reaction

was so strong and pervasive that the current chief executive officer decided to revert to what was then called the "heritage" widget, and all this in spite of the fact that the modification was minor from a design perspective.

What went wrong? A failure to link the design modification to the desired communication goals of the organization was one of the problems. The new design should have been introduced to internal audiences in a rigorous and appropriate manner before the external design launch. Secondly, the actual implementation emphasized the negative shape in the design. The highlighted "frown" was an unfortunate visual circumstance, to say the least. Lacking an appealing introduction, the new design was dismissed out of hand.

The relationships and emotional connections people have with symbols are complex. This makes it hard to create the right context for consensus-building and change, particularly when the goal is to reinvent or refresh an existing mark. You're often in a Catch-22 when working with cultural icons—criticized for pushing it too far, criticized for not pushing it far enough. You have to contend with the icon's history, its creators, its fans, and its far-reaching impact on the culture. This means that there are functional challenges as well as emotional ones. You have to learn to manage global timeframes; internal group-speak; differing work ethics, customs, and proper etiquette; and language barriers.

Understanding how people perceive symbols is crucial to the design process. Never assume anything—do your homework, and think. Once you comprehend the historic roots and values that have created the cultural links associated with an icon, you can apply the necessary tweaks without raising any alarms.

Our team was able to learn from previous mistakes. We introduced a fresh concept by building links to past designs, utilizing the Delta archives and a core group of employees we'd designated as "design ambassadors," who worked closely with us on the new modification. We created a site where all employees worldwide could go and learn about the new brand program, and this was accomplished before the larger public launch.

BRAND DEVELOPMENT

PROJECT

Lime Identity

DESIGNER

united*

CLIENT

Morris Street Partners

We won't take on a project unless there's an element of passion involved. To truly understand a brand you must eat, drink, and sleep it. You have to understand the way people behave, what they're wearing and feeling. You need to get into the heads of potential consumers.

We always throw out the client's creative brief and write one from scratch. We see the brief as a very dangerous item, like a ticket that can explode. Most are poorly written and can be the death sentence of a project. The best brief we were ever given wasn't so much a brief but a request: "I've got this sweet product. How do I share it with people?"

First, you have to get down and dirty with the client. It's crucial to absorb all of their knowledge about the product, to view the world through their eyes. In essence, you must become the client. This way you can take them into the world of the potential consumer, and show them the real people that are going to associate with their product. Once we become them, we flip it so that they can become us. We let them see the world through our lenses, throw out any

preconceived notions, and turn perceptions on their head. We argue and scream, we get each other's blood rushing, but since we have become each other, we go from being client and design firm to being partners with mutual respect for each other. In our insanity, we've taught each other empathy. We've learned that we have a common goal.

Lime brand identity program

We held several brainstorming sessions with the team from Morris Street Partners (MSP) to create the brand identity for Lime. We wanted to dive into their world of disability nonprofits, and to share weird, wild, and wonderful ideas on how they could present themselves. The ultimate goal, of course, was to differentiate MSP from the run of the pack. Brainstorming gave us a solid foundation upon which to build the project, beginning with an expedition in order to find the brand's name. We eventually chose Lime, since it was a unique and unexpected name within the world of disability nonprofits, easily accessible and hard to forget.

Brand name selected, trademarked, and registered, we began the creative process of developing an identity. We have never believed that inspiration cowers within a Mac, so we went back to our ABCs: pencils, markers, paints, crayons, and inks. We swiped visuals out of magazines, books, and street-and-alley trash: anything that caught our eye might have contained the germ of an idea. We posted our finds on all the walls of the studio, a hodge-podge of looming visuals to be absorbed—the creation of a living world called Lime.

We sought to immerse ourselves in the world of individuals with disabilities, imagining the hourly challenges and odd humiliations of those with cerebral palsy, blindness, dyslexia, and Down's syndrome. We spent time with hordes of special-needs students up and down the east coast of North America and, once back in the studio, after a couple of beers and barrels of coffee, we identified six creative directions. These were all pulled together onto boards, and then the Mac helped to bring them to life. After a solid week of work, we were ready to meet with the Lime team.

Once the direction was chosen, we set out to refine and process the look, feel, and attitude of the brand. We embarked upon another creative expedition in order to find the brand extensions, collateral, promotional materials, and guidelines. We discovered that one of the most important applications of the Lime brand was the web, so we created a site with full accessibility. This was designed to accommodate the special needs of viewers, who could adjust the size and color of the fonts, and, for those who were visually impaired, access the audio software we'd installed. To accomplish all of this, we partnered with 10:00am, an exceptional web-development company.

lime ®

disability
does not equal
disadvantage

> best practices **07**
industry standards
for people with disabilities
in the work place

lime
590 madison avenue
new york, ny 10022
t: 212 521 4469
f: 212 521 4099
www.lime.com

richard donovan
founder & chairman

lime
590 madison avenue
new york, ny 10022
212 521 4469
rich@lime.com

PROJECT

Ciao Bella Packaging

DESIGNER

Wallace Church, Inc.

CLIENT

Ciao Bella Gelato

A recently as 25 years ago, large corporations had robust internal design teams who joined with consultants in a true creative partnership. There was a shared understanding of what worked and what didn't, because we all spoke the same language. Today, there are still great creative minds running large corporate design departments, but, more often than not, marketing teams are calling the shots. Many of these marketers are nowhere near design-literate, and this is a sure sign of how different the playing field really is. Our first job is to train marketers to understand the value of design, so that they learn how to recognize the most effective strategies without equivocation. If there is one key to our success, it is our ability to build an affinity between the marketers and all the design-team members.

We have a firmly established 10-step process that we use for all our major engagements. The most important step involves converting the written positioning statement into what we call a "visual brand essence." Far too many positioning statements use the same cookie-cutter format, and this is detrimental. Better design happens more quickly and efficiently if there is an agreement as to the desired brand perceptions, and consensus on the visual tools that evoke them. After all, the consumer never sees the positioning statement. The consumer sees the colors, shapes, type styles, graphics, and design architecture that provoke their desires.

Looking through our project workbooks after each assignment is always very interesting. I can equate it to archaeologists searching for the bones of early man. Frequently, the most successful projects have the thinnest workbooks, since the first-phase concepts resemble what actually hits the market. That was certainly the case with the Ciao Bella design. This tiny importer of super-premium gelato and sorbetto wanted to bring a new product to the market that was twice as expensive as the leading super-premium ice creams. They defined their product as richly indulgent and utterly unique. And they could not afford photography!

However, we found success by breaking the rules. We replaced photography with iconography, making this the key brand mnemonic: a swirling icon communicates the rich indulgence of gelato while the snowflake symbolizes the icy refreshment of sorbetto. And, instead of building a brand around a distinct color, in line with our recommended design architecture, we went against the grain and utilized a wide color palette that the brand could own. The resulting image was "anti-big brand." Its look had a huge impact in speciality markets, and is now making an even bigger impression in the supermarket environment. Herein lies the lesson: never underestimate your audience's taste—the exact opposite of the Hollywood producer's philosophy. Never, ever dumb down your design so that it will appeal to the lowest common denominator. It is fine to be polarizing, disengaging those folks who are not the brand's target, so long as you delight the consumer who is in your sights, converting them into passionate brand advocates.

Design's greatest lesson is encapsulated by Milton Glaser's dictum, "Art is work." Remember that you are not designing for yourself, but for a specific target audience. Put yourself in their heads, delight them, provoke specific experiences. It's a lot harder to design for the everyday brand and still make it look special.

I once lowered our pricing in an effort to win a big project in a category where we had no direct experience. We undervalued our contribution, and that was a costly mistake. When we lose projects, our most common excuse is that we are too expensive. While this seems reasonable, what it really means is that we were not effective enough in proving the value that design brings to brand success.

Throughout my career, my unequivocal passion has been to prove design's return on investment. The research that we have generated to date proves, dollar-to-dollar, that design generates more bottom-line profit than advertising, or any other communications media. When we underbid an assignment, we underestimate design's value and we denigrate its worth.

Collectively, our goal in the industry is to replace fee-based compensation with a new compensation model based directly on the value that we provide. When designers can hold each other to this same standard, we become true partners with our clients, through all of the ups and downs that relationships entail, never again to be considered a service or a vendor whose value is wholly determined by the lowest bid.

RIGHT:
Final packaging.

MUSIC PACKAGING

PROJECT

A Ghost is Born

DESIGNER

Peter Buchanan-Smith

CLIENT

Wilco/ Nonsuch Records

My design process always begins with a list. This could include the box of My Boy toilet soap I found on a trip to Fez; Brian Eno's obsession with Photoshop; lots of exercise and the ensuing endorphin rush; the natural light in my office; wabi-sabi, hocus-pocus, and topsy-turvy; Chauncy Gardner; hard-boiled eggs, deviled eggs, poached eggs, par-boiled eggs and eggs benedict; Maira Kalman the designer; polka dots; a good book bag; the pale blue dot; brevity and infinity; black holes; suspense; Maira Kalman the human being; white space; Bodoni; smoking meat in my backyard; uniforms; Peter Sellers; a good breakfast cereal; bird guides; zero; the meek inheriting the earth; the elements of style; abstract patterns in nature (Peter Sellers again?); extravaganzas; obituaries; Scotland, Windex and science; round-the-world toothpaste; mediocrity; durability; my assistant Josef Reyes; manual lawnmowers; Raymond Carver's short stories; how objects can speak volumes; a messy desk; stand-up comedy; get-well cards; and my hero, Alexi Brodovitch (Brodovitch-schmodovitch).

Key:

Henry Miller, essay
Rick Moody, essay
Ben Porter, found poetry
Michael Schmelling, photography
Fred Tomaselli, artwork

Wilco, text and music

Stan Doty, front of house engineer (SD)
Mikael Jorgensen, keyboards (MJ)
Glenn Kotche, drums (GK)
Tony Margherita, manager (TM)
Frankie Marcoux, guitar tech (FM)
Jim O'Rourke, mix and production (JO)
John Stirratt, bass (JS)
Jason Tobias, production manager (JT)
Jeff Tweedy, guitar, vocals (JT)
Matt Zivich, stage tech (MZ)

Dan Nadel and Peter Buchanan-Smith,
editing and design (Permindex)

See Appendix VI.

A collaborative picture book about music. *The Wilco Book* documents the band at home, on tour, and in the recording studio, while expanding its ideas, philosophies, and working methods. With text by the band members, essays by Henry Miller and Rick Moody, and a compact disc of unreleased music, *The Wilco Book* is an unusual peek into the world of the re-invented group. It reads like a record.

PICTUREBOX, Inc.
$29.95 / Higher in Canada
ISBN 0-9746510-1-1

Wilco album cover

I would never have designed the Wilco album if I had not been a partner in the publication of *The Wilco Book*. The project, a visual analog to the band, was well underway when the band's lead singer, Jeff Tweedy, asked my business partner and I if we would like to design their new album cover—the very making of which we had been busily documenting. From the second we met them, I had experienced conflicting emotions: giddiness over the prospect of designing their album cover, and sheer terror at the possibility that I might be asked.

We had been working very closely with the photographer, Michael Schmelling, on the book project, so when the album gig kicked in, I turned to Michael's archive of photos and began to build from there. The design of the album took about three months, and during this time we were only able to meet with Jeff once. Wilco are from Chicago, and we were from New York, so 800 miles made all the

ABOVE:
The Wilco Book.

Following pages:
Sketches for *A Ghost is Born* album cover.

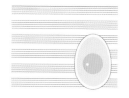

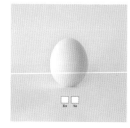

THE ESSENTIAL PRINCIPLES OF GRAPHIC DESIGN

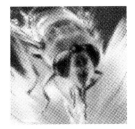
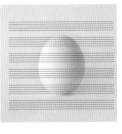

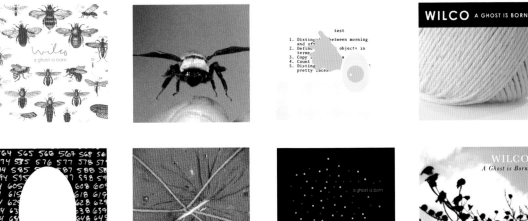

WILCO
A GHOST IS BORN

Wilco ≤ *a ghost is born*

79809-2

difference. During the two and a half months prior to our only meeting, we sent countless designs, all of which were never quite right. (Caveat to young designers everywhere: try not to blanket your client with endless solutions and don't bother to swaddle them in endless details, unless of course you worship the client, which can lead to actions and motivations that are highly unprofessional—maybe it's better to work for a client you are utterly indifferent to?)

In the shuffle of all these designs—some bad, some good, some plain awful—the band finally decided what to name the album. Soon after I received word, I instinctively reached for a copy of my first book, *Speck,* flipped to the title page, and lo and behold, there it was: the egg. In my excitement, I quickly mocked it up and jpegged it to Jeff, and word came flying back that it wasn't quite right. Back to the drawing board.

A month passed, leaving in its wake a trail of dead, rejected designs. The deadline was rapidly approaching and we still had nothing. Jeff was scheduled to stop by our studio on his way back from mastering the album in London, and there was a last-minute request by Wilco management to resuscitate the egg concept. In walked a jetlagged Jeff, and, in less than 30 minutes, the final design was decided, and an egg was born. It's funny how all at once anything is possible, and yet everything is impossible.

My biggest mistakes can always be attributed to my fears. Unless they are catastrophic, mistakes by nature are fleeting. They are eventually set right and recover quite nicely through the passage of time. I look back on my mistakes with a certain amount of adoration, for they've made me who I am. Still, the hardest mistake to bounce back from is the one that hurts someone else. Doing or saying something to deflate an individual's confidence is the worst mistake that I can think of.

STRUCTURAL DESIGN

PROJECT

Bottle Design

DESIGNER

Branko Lucic, Nonobject Inc.

CLIENT

Vertikal Vodka

At Nonobject, we do not believe in "processed" design. We have an evolving methodology that is almost process-less. It is important to remember that every client is unique and deserves a unique approach, and that each project has its own unique set of business and design parameters. We pay the utmost attention to the mastery involved in preserving original design intent, and we do this by making mistakes. Mistakes are important because they lead to development—one mistake always leads to another, and all the repairs done along the way result in a successful project. By applying our methods consistently, we've learned to move nimbly and risk more through innovation and expression.

When I first started working, I used to sketch a lot, but that changed six years ago. Now, I think first in order to resolve design challenges before I touch a pencil or a computer. I can often "see" ideas in my mind, and this is where I now develop almost everything. After the meditation phase, I will quickly sketch my ideas in order to test and validate my thinking. It is only then that I will approach the computer. It is very important for me to highlight that I was

RIGHT:
Vertikal Vodka bottle design.

VERTIKAL premium vodka. 700ml e, alc 40% vol.

+ made with highest quality natural spring water vodavoda from banja vrujci source. bottled by si&si company product of serbia and montenegro.

schooled in the old, analog way of the "artist." One of the things
I do not encourage is to immediately start thinking and designing
on the computer. I believe you must be proficient in tangible
art techniques in order to be able to meaningfully transfer
your thoughts through your hand to paper.

Vertikal Vodka

One of our favorite projects was for Vertikal Vodka. We gave the
brand flesh, blood, personality, and soul. We gave it a name and
a look, and put so much of ourselves into it that it acquired DNA.
In an oversaturated market of premium and ultra-premium
vodka brands, we sought to stir up new emotional responses and
connections through our design approach. We wanted to push
the limits while being practical—keeping in mind the cost
implications, engineering complexity, and manufacturability.
We asked ourselves questions: Could we make a bottle without
a neck? Is this impossible? And our relentless questing gave birth
to Vertikal Vodka, the first neckless bottle, consciously designed
for reuse as an elegant vase.

Whether you are designing a bottle for a water beverage or a vodka
product, you must understand the target market for the product.
Then you must investigate the available production techniques, as
well as the limitations, the energy efficiency, the labeling strategies,
and the warehousing (fulfillment/shipment) processes. Once
you understand the processes, you can challenge the limitations,
particularly the engineering. It's only via a thoroughly informed
perspective that you'll be able to deliver true innovation and the
maximum consumer experience.

ABOVE:
Detail, Vertikal Vodka bottle design.

RIGHT:
Vertikal Vodka bottle cap.

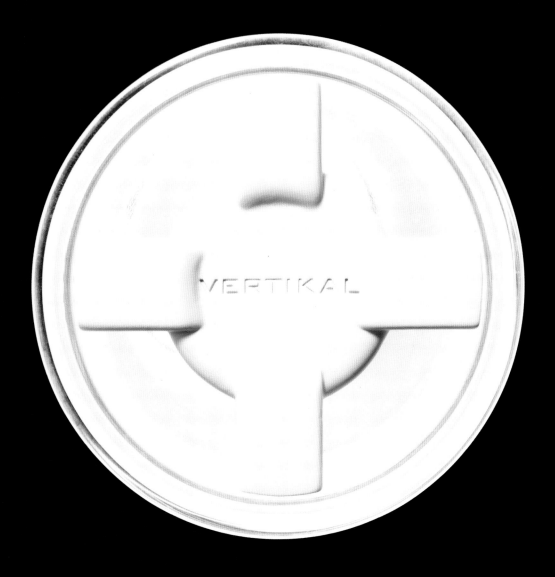

PROJECT

ClearRx

DESIGNER

Deborah Adler, Milton Glaser Inc.

CLIENT

Target Corporation

Assignments and ideas reside in my head for a long while before I begin working. I problem-solve and strategize before the pencil even scratches paper. I spend a great length of time researching and listening. Once I hear the necessary click, I bring out the sketchpad or hop onto the computer and make it all happen. I usually work until I begin to lose interest, and that's when I slink off to allow the hot idea to cool down a bit before I add the necessary refinements. Eventually, I end up with two or three solutions that are worth presenting.

The ClearRx project began as a student project (SafeRx) and burgeoned into a major innovation for the pharmaceutical/medical industry.

These are the initial sketches from my days as a student. I originally wanted the front of the bottle to maintain its curved shape, in order to retain its familiarity. I soon discovered that I had to immerse myself in the world of prescription packaging to resolve any problems.

RIGHT:
Initial student sketches: criticisms of existing pharmaceutical packaging with notes and suggestions for improvement.

Prototype bottles.

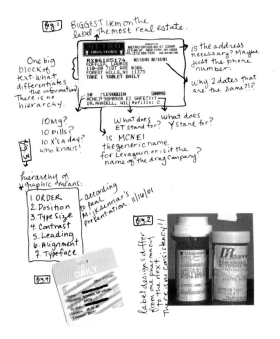

[Fig. 1] BIGGEST Item on the label. The most real estate.

METRO DRUG STORES
METRO DRUGS 880 ST. CORP.
13 E 9th ST, NEW YORK, NY 10003
Ph. (212) 988-7325
RX#6125174   02/18/01 02/18/01
KOPPLER, LAURIE
110-28 71ST AVE #306.
FOREST HILLS, NY 11375
TAKE 1 TABLET DAILY

10   LEVAQUIN   500MG
MCNEI 98P092B. ET SAFETY:Y
DR. WANDELL, WIL Refills: 2

is the address necessary? Maybe just the phone number.

Why 2 dates that are the same?!?

One big block of text. What differentiates the information? There is no hierarchy.

10Mg? 10 Pills? 10 X's a day? Who Knows!

What does ET stand for? what does Y stand for?

IS MCNEI the generic name for Levaquin or is it the name of the drug company?

hierarchy of ★graphic means:
1. ORDER
2. Position
3. Type Size
4. Contrast
5. Leading
6. Alignment
7. Typeface

— according to paul M. Kenner's presentation. 11/16/01

[Fig. 2]

label designs differ from one pharmacy to the next. There is no consistency!!

[Fig. 4]
DAILY
Value:
SCHOOL OF VISUAL ARTS

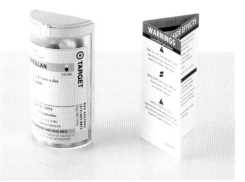

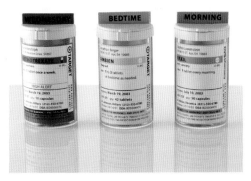

WEDNESDAY   BEDTIME   MORNING

[FIG. 5]
NEITHER WARNING WORKS!

Some warnings are printed out dirctly on the label. Worse than stickers because you don't pay attention. Text can come misaligned making it impossible to read.

→ Very difficult to read the red and orange labels against an orange bottle. It does not draw attention to itself.

THIS IS THE LAST REFILL FOR THIS PRESCRIPTION

TAKE MEDICATION ON AN EMPTY STOMACH

FOR EXTERNAL USE ONLY

TAKE WITH FOOD

WE OWE YOU

DO NOT TAKE WITH NITRATES

DO NOT TAKE WITH ASPIRIN

Black type does not Contrast enough with the background color.

[FIG. 6]

DRUG NAME

LABEL

LABEL

LOGO
①
⑪
⑪⑦

Above are a number of my prototype bottles. I am not an industrial designer, so I formed them out of plexi-tubing and dollhouse materials. I applied colors to each of the labels in order to personalize medications for each member of a household. This alone would have prevented my grandmother from accidentally taking my grandfather's medication.

I wanted these bottles to be user-friendly. The new label contained space to include any information the pharmacist needed to inscribe. When people opened their cabinets, they could see to whom the medicine belonged and how to take it, just by glancing at it.

I brought my prototypes to the United States Federal Drug Administration (FDA) with the high hopes of making them a federal standard. The FDA was supportive of the notion, but their hands were tied because every state had its own Board of Pharmacy to dole out approvals. Undaunted, I soon realized that the fastest way to inject my product into the national bloodstream was through a national pharmacy.

I decided to contact Target, an excellent platform for my product. Target is committed to its customers and always goes the extra mile to create consumer loyalty. Luckily, Target is also committed to great design—it is the essence of the brand. I was convinced that Target would be willing to take a risk with my innovative product, and I was proved correct. Working together, we polished my ideas and developed the ClearRx system.

The long collaborative effort included Target's technology, pharmacy, operations, training, and marketing teams. I worked closely with Klaus Rosburg, an industrial designer, to create synergy between the bottle and the label. We developed label, bottle, and card designs that achieved my initial goals and met the real-world needs of patients and pharmacists.

My original plan to color-code labels was translated into color-coded rings. The final label is very close to my original vision.

We also designed a patient information card, summarizing common uses, potential side effects, and a plethora of useful information, which is tucked in the back of the bottle. Milton Glaser and I updated the 25 most important warning and instructional icons.

RIGHT:
The final bottle design.

Iconography

  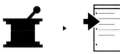

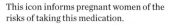 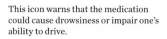

This icon informs pregnant women of the risks of taking this medication.

This icon warns that the medication could cause drowsiness or impair one's ability to drive.

This icon expresses the importance of reading all the instructions before taking the medication.

Target A Guest

AMOXICILLIN 500MG

Capsule   Generic for: Amoxil

Take one capsule by mouth three times daily for 10 days

qty: **30**

refills: **No**

Dr. C Wilson

disp: 03/17/06   TST

mfr: NDC: 00781-2613-05

(877)798-2743 $\overset{R}{\underset{X}{}}$ 6666056-1375

⊙®TARGET PHARMACY
900 Nicollet Mall
Minneapolis, MN 55403

PATIENT INFO CARD

INNOVATION

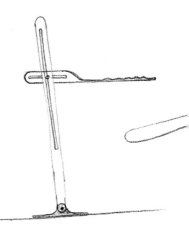

PROJECT

LEAF Light

DESIGNER

Yves Behar, Fuse Project

CLIENT

Herman Miller

Fuse Project developed an advanced, mechanically complex LED task light called LEAF. Ever since its debut at the 2006 International Contemporary Furniture Fair in New York, it has rapidly become an iconic product. It is part of the Museum of Modern Art's vast collection, and has garnered numerous green awards. More than four years of engineering and design development resulted in this radical product: a light with a minimal physicality containing a maximal capacity to expulse light. It is the first product of its kind to offer illumination that can be altered according to the consumer's choice, from warm mood lighting to cool and workmanlike illumination.

Our challenge lay primarily in the design. How could we create a product that housed within its very functionality a dual use, yet managed to retain the high design standards we held ourselves up to? We had to combine innovation with sustainable design, and apply new technologies.

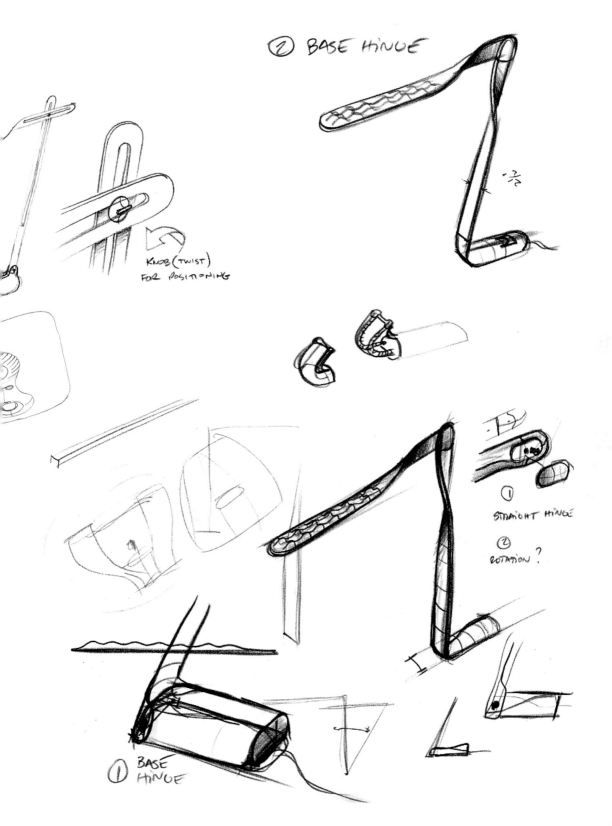

② BASE HINGE

KNOB (TWIST)
FOR POSITIONING

① STRAIGHT HINGE

② ROTATION ?

① BASE
HINGE

Strategy

To develop a detailed plan and bold-faced statement, relying upon brand/product strategy and positioning, naming and identity, communications, packaging, and web presence in order to further illuminate the product for the client.

Technology

We designed and engineered our own LED light bulb—a self-contained, replaceable LED board and heat sink that offered a high lumen output, so fewer bulbs were required. Extensive engineering research resulted in the integration of a heat sink into the top arm of the LEAF lamp, allowing the bulbs to remain cool to the touch. For a task lamp, this was of paramount importance, for it was necessary to be able to physically move the arm to achieve directional light.

Transformative

LEAF is the only LED lamp to provide dual lighting choices for the consumer. Bright white light can help workers focus on their tasks, while warm and friendly light can serve to ease the atmosphere while a room is illuminated. The sculptural shape of LEAF embodies its transformative qualities. The 180-degree hinge allows the user to direct the arm at their whim, in order to cast a warm or bright light.

Interactive

A special user interface was developed to control and adjust the LEAF. The user can trigger specialized software that manages the LED tone and luminosity, by running their fingers across the arc molded onto the base. Dual sides of the arc control the differing qualities of light.

PREVIOUS PAGES:
Development sketches of the LEAF mechanism.

LEFT:
LEAF light from above.

BELOW:
The LED series, showing the different bulbs that allow the lamp to provide both warm and cool light.

Environmental

LEDs use 40 percent less energy than compact fluorescent bulbs and last 10 times longer. Thirty-seven percent of LEAF is comprised of recycled materials, while the material content (steel, aluminum, plastic) is 95 percent recyclable to the end of its life. The slim form of the product uses fewer materials and is designed for disassembly.

Aesthetics

The elegant sculptural form provides the aesthetics and functionality. The slender design is simple yet expressive, enhancing its environment through a natural yet fluid form.

Through the integration of compact LEDs within a twisting, stamped aluminum blade, LEAF presents the thinnest profile. The dynamic upper arm twists 90 degrees, allowing three functions: the transition from a LED horizontal light area into vertical structure hinge point; the dissipation of generated heat; and the retractable movements of the horizontal arm which permit dramatic ambient lighting. The result is an inimitable form that uses few materials and requires little assembly.

Bottom line

LEAF accrued large orders and mass-market appeal for both high-end and popular design/lifestyle retailers.

LEFT:
LEAF light in profile .

ABOVE:
LEAF packaging.

TYPOGRAPHY

Font Design

Hoefler & Frere-Jones

Hoefler & Frere-Jones

All typefaces demand a balance between technical performance and visual style. The ultimate challenge facing a typeface designer is to determine what is worth doing. I think this is unique to this type of design, for it can transpire without an external brief. A designer can't design a book cover without a manuscript, or dream up an advertising campaign without a client, but a typeface can be summoned *ex nihilo*. Countless hours have been devoted to projects that aren't worthwhile in the long run. The best type designers are those who ruthlessly edit their work, paring it down to the bone.

Both Tobias [Frere-Jones] and I [Jonathan Hoefler] were drawn to typography as adolescents because we thought typefaces were neat; we loved their connotative power—whether it was subtle things, like "Gill Sans looks somehow British," or the more obvious references in font styles that suggest digital readouts or automobile chrome. When we entered the field, it became clear to us that type design wasn't just about making things look appealing, it was

BELOW:
Archer type specimen sheet.

ssible by your c

made this our mc

Jote

s filled with prom

year we've a spe

ions of one of ou

y-year career has

e of a mere comr

ly commissioned

iversary.

r participants en

to the arts throug

the most excitin

his new work, wh

explored resource nable in the ii

nponents UL te

Offer

exclu

the G

ISLAN

guest

beau

are in

villas

regio

ot Mirror
a Large)

le Sconce
le Sconce
le Sconce
lder
ble size)

vel Ring
red Shelf
estanding)

A

SCIE

about the challenge of solving problems. Every aspect of design is a conscious decision, and the delicate interplay between these decisions is what makes a typeface great. Pick your favorite font and try to articulate what makes it special. It's probably not "the serifs" or "the lowercase g," but rather an ineffable characteristic that emerges from the careful consideration given to every aspect of the design. After all, a font is only as good as the designer who uses it. Force yourself to articulate why you're creating a new typeface in the first place. Someone's idea of marrying two faces to offer a host of differing voices gave the world its first pairing of roman and italic. Someone desiring to change the weight of a typeface to grant emphasis to certain words produced the world's first bold. The best ideas, the ones that last the longest, have a certain reference point, and a pondering of past work is the key to the creation of the radical.

Knowledge of history and a facility with technology are crucial in this business, along with good old-fashioned patience. The computer fosters impatience with its speed and overall slickness. The real act of typeface design is not in the drawing but in the looking. Making the letters is the easy part; evaluating the results is far more difficult. This is where patience can be applied beneficially. What works for one typeface may not work for another. A great deal of the designer's work consists of brokering a set of arrangements that are invisible to the reader.

Robert Bringhurst famously observed that type design is an art in which the microscopic and macroscopic constantly converge. That's very true for the way in which typefaces are developed: at every stage, it's not merely letterforms that are being examined, but the ways in which they work together.

We usually start a typeface by drawing a handful of characters that suggest the general direction that the design will follow. A capital H and O embody the basic distinction between flat and round letters, and the lowercase letters n o p h a will describe the overall dimensions of a font—its flat and round shapes, its width (and the degree to which its character widths will differ from one another), the height of its lowercase letters, and the lengths of its projecting strokes (a descender in the p, and an ascender in the h). The lowercase a is often a telltale character, since it can be

Our Favorite Typefaces and Why

Mercury: I drew the display faces that served as the "seed crystal" for the project. Tobias developed these into a much more comprehensive family of text faces. Our past experience nurtured our creations—for me, in magazine typography; for Tobias, in newspaper text.

Gotham: This began with a specific piece of lettering: the 8th Avenue façade of the Port Authority Bus Terminal in New York City. Extrapolating from these 15 letters to a set of 26 was straightforward enough, but continuing on to the figures, the lowercase, the punctuation, and then italics—a range of eight weights, and a set of four

different widths—was a genuine challenge. The further afield a character was from these capitals, the more challenging it was to draw. The capitals look as if their strokes have consistent thickness, but the lowercase cannot. The ruthless policy of rounds and flats that works in wider faces doesn't really serve condensed faces very well.

constructed in any number of ways—most fundamentally, it can be a single-storey "ball-and-stick" design, or the more traditional two-storey shape. The size of its enclosed aperture will inform the proportions of other characters, such as e and g, and the way in which its topmost stroke terminates will become a theme for other related characters: a "ball terminal" here will recur in the letters f g r y, and perhaps later in the numbers. Taken together, its topmost and bottom-most strokes will suggest the kinds of gestures that the font will make—whether they're introverted or extroverted, and how fussy their details will be. It often takes several more characters to establish concretely that the design is following the right path: some designs start out with a beautiful a, but can't seem to accommodate a sympathetic g.

Once these characters are drawn, they're proofed on paper at a range of sizes, and in every possible context. At this point we're trying to establish some generalities about the design, both visual and emotional: as important as its color and fit, we're curious about the sorts of feelings the font conveys. Also at this point, we'll be looking at every possible combination of characters, to spot inconsistencies in the design or problems that should be addressed at a more fundamental level.

Once we're happy with the result, the rest of the project is essentially a matter of continuing to expand the character set in small steps, and repeating the process of reviewing the results, to see how these new characters change the big picture. (There are about 600 characters in the average font these days, so it's a series of slow and steady steps.) It's not uncommon for a single character to bring the whole underlying structure crashing down—think about the 8-shaped grid on a digital watch, for example, and consider its difficulties in displaying a letter M. Even in its most advanced stages, typeface design is a matter of constantly brokering agreements between individual characters and the font as a whole, and it's not until the complete design is finished that you ever really know what it's going to look like.

LEFT:
Sketches and markups for Mercury.

Type specimen sheets for Gotham.

Typefaces We Try to Avoid

Helvetica: Helvetica is reputed as the pinnacle of legibility, beauty, and neutrality. But no typeface can live up to its reputation, not even Helvetica itself, for it can be viewed as the off-white paint your landlord chose for your new apartment.

Arial: This is Helvetica without the good parts. The result is a typeface that lazily declares "Leave me alone, this is the best I could do." It's the paint from the 99-cent store that makes you long for the landlord's choice of voluptuous off-white.

Times Roman: Decades of modification and adaptation have erased what little charm it once had. What remains stares back at you from the page, both grudging and reluctant. It is the movie star who is bland and wooden, but inexplicably gets all the best roles, sleeps with all the ingénues and commands $20,000,000 a picture.

Bodoni: There are many interpretations and revivals of Giambattista Bodoni's work, some dull, some sparkling. It is one of the easiest typefaces and is always horribly misused, for what is delicate in a headline will look feeble in the text. Bodoni is the blind date who went to an Ivy League college and looks sharp in a suit, only he's a finicky eater, wears far too much cologne, and can't stop bragging about his car.

Peignot: There is something unique about a design that can so potently evoke an exact moment in the past. The price for that special ability, though, is that it is trapped in its time and doomed to anachronism in our own. It's the yellow turtleneck that looked great on Steve McQueen, but draped over your body makes you look like an idiot.

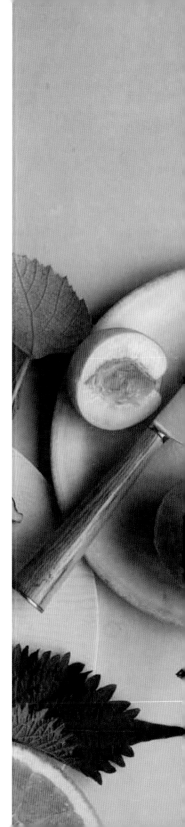

PROJECT

Martha Stewart Brand Identity

DESIGNER

Stephen Doyle, Doyle Partners

CLIENT

Martha Stewart Living Omnimedia

The brand value statement is a very helpful guide for shaping a new identity. It was a little long for my taste, so I highlighted some of the words that were most helpful. We paid constant attention to whether our design was an actual embodiment and visualization of some of the words in the statement.

Here is the original:
"The handmade, the homemade, the artful, the innovative, the practical, the contemporary, and the beautiful."

We are not just about lifestyle, but about essential tools for modern living. Not just about the how-to, but about the why-to. We aim to inspire the creativity that can transform homemaking into domestic arts, or a simple dinner into an occasion—filling our lives with a little more quality, a little more permanence, a little more

lasting beauty. We are not just a company, but a laboratory for ideas and a community celebrating the art of the everyday.

And here is the revised version:
"The handmade, the homemade, the artful, the innovative, the practical, the contemporary, and the beautiful... a little more quality, a little more permanence, a little more lasting beauty."

There was much discussion and heated debate over whether the rebrand name should be "Martha Stewart" or "MarthaStewart." The thinking was that the lack of a word space would help transform a person's name into a corporation, but the argument against it lay in how it would be read in press releases and newspapers. One question was paramount: what was the overlying subject foremost in the minds of the consumer, the woman, or the corporation?

Names maintain an aura; they can nurture tremendous power. We could never escape the high passion of a certain individual's ideas concerning Martha Stewart. Those two seemingly benign words carry a lot of emotional weight. Adding anything to MARTHA and STEWART, such as a logo emblem or some kind of abstract flourish, would have diminished it. Due to Martha's prominence in the world, and pre-eminence in her categories, we were forced to rely upon the power of her name to the exclusion of everything else—no trees, leaves, spoons, or big Ms. We had to create a distinctive and proprietary way to present the words, meanwhile dodging the word space bullet, whose differing camps were quickly polarizing. I kept thinking of my favorite photograph of Martha. She is out by her barn wearing a barn jacket, and she is walking with a handmade wreath of orange, yellow, and red maple leaves. The movement and color bring this image to life, and I can recall the pleasant surprise of seeing the wreath in motion, swinging actually, blurry, and bright, and joyful. It seemed natural to transform the Martha Stewart name into a wreath and, naturally, it was difficult to pull off.

I struggled with a condensed sans serif in Illustrator, searching for a contemporary feel, and I got the words to work beautifully in a circle. Twice. It looked great, but it said, "Martha Stewart Martha Stewart." This put me in mind of the 1970s sitcom,

Mary Hartman, Mary Hartman, which was about a dimwitted young woman with red hair in two enormous braids—this was not the proper frame of reference. After days of finger-gnawing frustration, trying to convince myself that this wreath thing was on the right track, I attempted a pencil drawing with wide letters, the "Martha" swinging around on the tip of a circle, and the "Stewart" swinging around on the bottom. The visual reference altered immediately from a wreath to a coin. This new idea hit upon the "quality, permanence, and lasting beauty" part of the equation, subtly suggesting that this public company was valuable, dependable, and bankable. After all, nothing suggests "worth" like currency and coins. The Greeks were minting coins with arcs of type around the edges as early as the fourth century BC. That's what I call durability!

Now that the idea consisted of carved or minted letters in a coin/ wreath form, I began by hand-drawing the letters in order to get a better sense of the character and the radial stems. We began with the letterforms of Trajan, but this quickly evolved into a version of Optima due to our rigorous research. We wanted the letterforms to reproduce in miniscule applications, like buttons or tacks, which would maintain its handsomeness when shown either carved or embossed. Based on this font, we drew it repeatedly in order to grow away from a rigidity, adding an organic sense of "handmade, homemade, and artful" to the letterforms themselves.

Time and again I've seen this logo criticized on design blogs due to its imperfections. My reaction is, "Yes, exactly! It is not meant to be perfect." In order to discern whether or not the letters were exactly imperfect in a correct manner, I actually carved the type into a disk of plaster. I imagined plaques that could be used in-store, incised with these 13 important letters.

After reading the brand statement for the millionth time, it occurred to me that our goal as craftsmen was for this logo to be seen as equally Arts & Crafts movement (twentieth century—the handmade and artful) and Wedgewood (mid-eighteenth century— lasting beauty). The circular configuration offered the idea of community: a group of 13 come together, circle-shaped, conjoined, providing energy and movement as they coalesce into something bigger than they could ever be individually.

LEFT:
Product packaging.
Logo pattern used for endpapers.

ABOVE:
Logo being carved into stone.

FOLLOWING PAGES:
Logo in use on a range of Martha Stewart publications.

Gardening 101

Arranging Flowers

Halloween eggs carnival glass apples & gratins hardware-store décor

asta glossary stylish banquettes dark chocolate marbleized valentines

decoupage projects a kitchen makeover making pillows forcing bulbs

za on the grill versatile pegboard cheesecakes a fresh look at silk flowers

mp, slaws, and quiches campanulas lunch on a rose farm wirework crafts

IDEAS > INSPIRATION > UPGRADES > FIXES > FINDS > SHORT CUTS > CHECKLISTS > BREAKTHROUGHS

ON | DISCOVER YOUR POWER ZONE | WHAT TO DO WITH TOFU | LIFE LESSONS FROM HERB SCHOOL | UNTIE THE KNOTS

EVERYDAY FOOD

EVERYDAY FOOD

EVERYDAY FOOD

EVERYDAY FOOD

VERYDAY FOOD

ERYDAY FOOD

GOOD THINGS FOR ORGANIZING

MARTHA STEWART'S HORS D'OEUVRES HANDBOOK

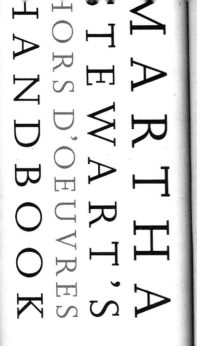

MARTHA STEWART

GARDENING

MARTHA STEWART

MARTHA STEWART LIVING VOLUME 1

MARTHA STEWART

MARTHA STEWART LIVING VOLUME 2

MARTHA STEWART

MARTHA STEWART LIVING VOLUME 3

MARTHA STEWART

ENVIRONMENTAL DESIGN

PROJECT

Morgan Square

DESIGNER

Bennett Peji, Bennett Peji Design

CLIENT

National City Redevelopment Agency and the National City Downtown PBID

I was hired to plan and lead an aggressive identity makeover for the entire downtown district of National City, in San Diego County, California. We conducted community workshops that resulted in bold new names and graphics. The identity system included the positioning/thematic platform, logo and design usage guidelines, stationery systems, information kiosks, banners, way-finding systems, street furniture, architectural concepts, and monumental gateway signage.

ABOVE:
Initial logo sketches.

MORGAN
SQUARE

THE HEART OF SOUTH BAY

I still maintain the same business model I began with 20 years ago, though a lot of the terminology has changed, and the depth of research has become significantly greater. I now include ethnographic research, economic impact studies, community design charrettes, targeting, and positioning in order to determine the touch points for a brand, and a well-developed communications

ABOVE:
Identity for Morgan Square.

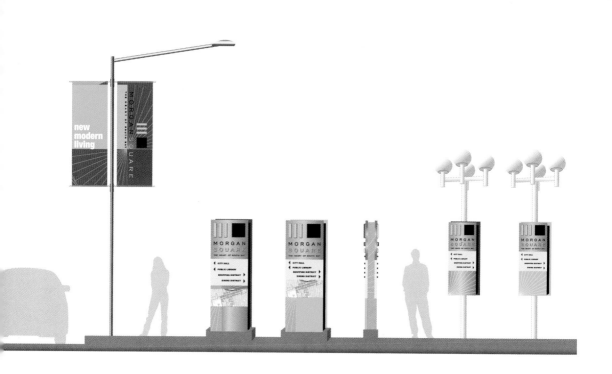

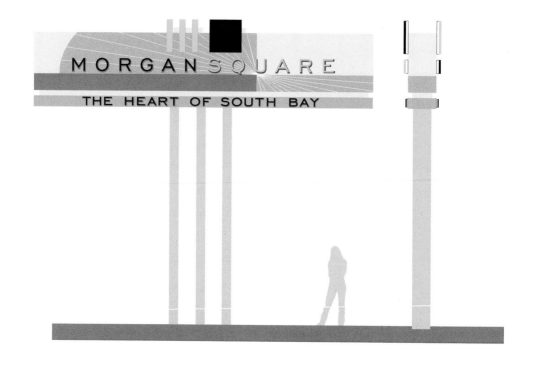

matrix. I work closely with my clients and stakeholders in order to establish important themes that:

- Create a distinct and authentic sense of place
- Weave together places, businesses, people, and their stories
- Help restore civic pride
- Focus on the revival of buildings, street blocks, and the neighborhood
- Stimulate economic development
- Cultivate community interaction

When the public debates about improving my community occurred, I wanted to be able to lead the conversation; merely following along did not interest me. This required strategically choosing where to engage in that conversation, because the debate was so broad and unwieldy. For me, it was about refocusing my business on district branding. All of the things I've learned about positioning products and services, I'd brought to bear for the good of the community; it was crucial for me to make an impact at that juncture. Remember that all of the art, design, and culture that we choose to leave behind will tell those in the future who we were and what we stood for.

I'm rarely involved in print production implementation, so I'm often shielded from the classic design mistakes. But I think it's helpful to mention that all mistakes revolve around three words: "burnout," "money," and "liability." Prevention of burnout requires the establishment of proper client and project management; prevention of money woes requires the creation of substantial fiduciary guidelines; and constructing a firewall against the onslaught of liability exposure claims requires a forward-thinking investment in proper insurance, such as "errors and omissions," in order to guarantee protection for your original ideas and designs.

This is a lot to take in. But you could take comfort in this bit of simple advice: surround yourself with good people who tell good stories about other good people. This means that you must become deeply engaged within a community of generous-minded individuals, who find true pleasure in the age-old art of storytelling. They usually have all the right answers, and, purely by association, good things are bound to follow.

PROJECT

Northern Arizona University Wayfinding

DESIGNER

David Gibson, 212 Associates

CLIENT

Northern Arizona University

We designed the new wayfinding strategies and signage for Northern Arizona University (NAU) in collaboration with EDAW landscape architects. This was a sustainable project that facilitated navigation through the NAU campus and enriched the day-to-day experience of the university community.

In 2004, NAU embarked on a series of infrastructure improvements to bring the campus up to date, functionally and visually. These improvements included new landscaping, sidewalks, walls, lighting, and signs. The university, located 7,000ft (2,134m) above sea level, sought harmonization with its beautiful, harsh, and ecologically sensitive desert mountain environs.

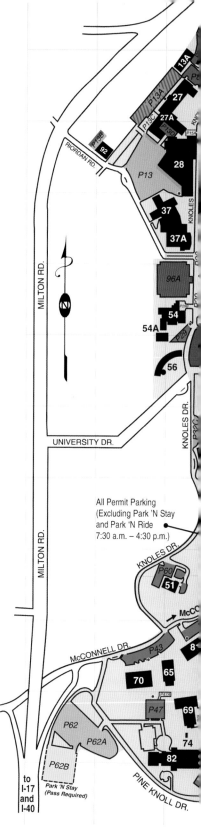

The Design Process

So often a part of larger building projects, wayfinding and signage are mini-construction projects in and of themselves. The process we use at 212 Associates is significantly more detailed than the typical branding or print project, due primarily to its size and complexity. Just look at what it comprises: the need for a wide range of specifications (layout, typography, messaging, materials, sign locations, fabrication, and mounting methods); the coordination of numerous partners, stakeholders, and consultants; and added design considerations, such as the environment in which the sign will be placed, and how exterior signage will fare in unfavorable weather.

We work closely with client and project teams to uncover the hidden logic of information. Whether we're working on a hospital, streetscape, office tower, or waterfront esplanade, we define the project's physical and communication needs before we visualize them as design solutions. In other words, each new project begins with planning and strategy.

Research and analysis:
In this phase of the planning process, we conduct user interviews, focus groups, and site surveys to understand the operational requirements. In any new construction, we review architectural plans and analyze anticipated circulation patterns, such as pedestrian traffic flow.

Strategy:
This is the functional framework of the system, explaining how it will provide information and directions through a particular space. We then develop a preliminary outline, or "family," of the types of signs that will be required, and establish the design objectives of the signage.

We begin with schematic design, as a print designer would. We finalize sign types, decide locations, and create mock-ups in order to visualize the signs in three dimensions.

Schematic design:
We select key sign types and explore design alternatives. These variations use different language forms, materials palettes, color and type systems, and content variations. All options conform to the wayfinding strategy, yet emphasize different approaches to content and visual vocabulary.

Programming:
With sign types established and circulation paths anticipated, our wayfinding experts plot key locations and create a message schedule database indicating the specific words to be laid out on each sign. Complete messages will be recorded and final locations are noted. By the end of this stage, we calculate the preliminary sign-fabricating budget.

Design development:
We develop the approved schematic design, finalize it, and seek client approval. To ensure the integrity of our designs, we coordinate with architects and engineers, and discuss power, load, and structural issues. Finally, we revisit the sign-fabrication budget, as the sign quantities are fixed and the details are resolved to everyone's satisfaction.

Now that the design is complete, we prepare for production.

Construction documentation:
We develop construction-intent drawings for all the approved sign types. In the documents, we address final sign layouts, elevations, and fabrication details to define the design intent, and provide sufficient information for bidding and construction purposes. We then assemble the final programming materials, which are submitted to fabricators, who use them to develop estimates.

Bid phase:
We identify and contact qualified fabricators, typically holding a pre-bid conference meeting in order to discuss the construction-intent documents or answer any questions. Throughout the process, we provide clarifications as necessary and help the client review and evaluate submitted bids.

To complete the implementation of a wayfinding and signage program, we help the client oversee its fabrication and installation. The fabricator may produce a mock-up of a sign or signage element so that we can evaluate the physical quality of production and materials.

Construction administration:
We attend pre-construction meetings to clarify the construction-intent documents. During construction, we conduct visits to the fabricator's workshop to review materials, colors, samples, etc. After fabrication is complete, we provide onsite supervisory assistance during installation.

Throughout the planning and strategy process, we had to take into account the unique conditions of the high-altitude climate. We opted to employ the principles of sustainable design. Our goals were to minimize invasive construction, integrate signage into the natural environment, and utilize eco-friendly materials.

We conducted a thorough planning process, requiring us to work closely with EDAW, university planners, and facilities staff, seeking to determine the appropriate areas for pathways and landscape enhancements. Once the wayfinding strategies were approved, we developed a family of sign types—identification, directional, orientational, and regulatory— and the designers drew up the location plan. We discussed issues of nomenclature and identity, deciding what places should be called and whether or not the school's logo should appear.

The programming largely complete, we set to work on the signage, drawing inspiration from Arizona's gorgeous landscape, complemented by the brilliant blue skies and the rich industrial history of Flagstaff, the famous town nearby. We reined in our aesthetic choices, keeping in mind the fluctuations of the often harsh weather—brutal snowstorms, high-speed winds, heavy monsoon rains, and powerful sunlight. In order to enhance visibility, we specified high-contrast white lettering against deep blue fields, and, mindful of the driving winds and snowfall, formatted layouts in a vertical fashion and mounted signs higher than usual.

We wanted to minimize the environmental impact, so we selected a variety of sustainable construction materials. For the bases, we used natural sandstone that had been shipped from a local quarry, and for the panels we used steel and UV-resistant porcelain. We also specified mechanical hardware, as opposed to toxic adhesives, whenever possible. This resulted in a comprehensive signage system which was resistant to fading, required minimal maintenance, and was durable enough to withstand the blows delivered by the environment.

We gave the university staff a signage design manual, containing layouts and specifications for all sign types, which would enable them to extend and update the program as needed.

RIGHT:
Initial presentation, wayfinding scheme number 1.

FOLLOWING PAGES:
The final designs, with notes on technical specifications.

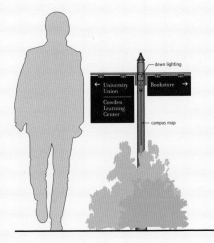

down lighting

← University
Union

Cowden
Learning
Center

Bookstore →

campus map

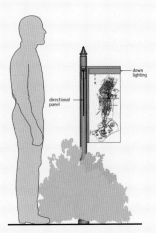

down
lighting

directional
panel

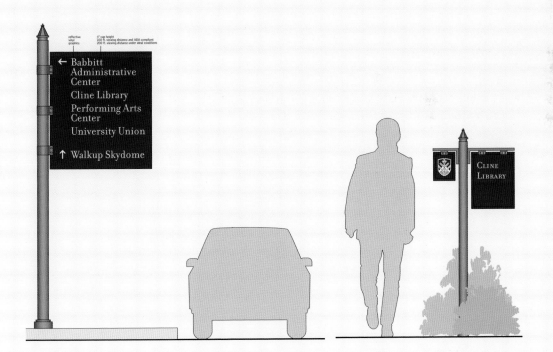

reflective
vinyl
graphics

4" cap height
100 ft. viewing distance and ADA compliant
200 ft. viewing distance under ideal conditions

← Babbitt
Administrative
Center

Cline Library

Performing Arts
Center

University Union

↑ Walkup Skydome

CLINE
LIBRARY

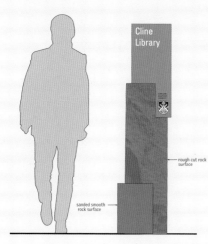

Cline
Library

sanded smooth
rock surface

rough cut rock
surface

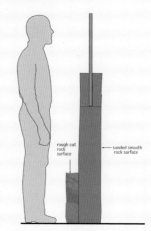

rough cut
rock
surface

sanded smooth
rock surface

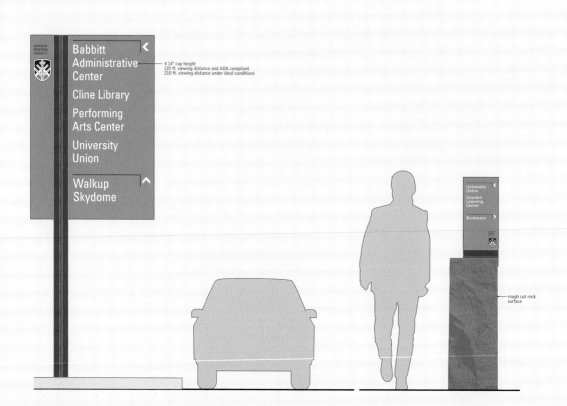

NORTHERN
ARIZONA
UNIVERSITY

Babbitt
Administrative
Center

Cline Library

Performing
Arts Center

University
Union

Walkup
Skydome

4 14" cap height
110 ft. viewing distance and ADA compliant
210 ft. viewing distance under ideal conditions

University
Union

Cowden
Learning
Center

Bookstore

rough cut rock
surface

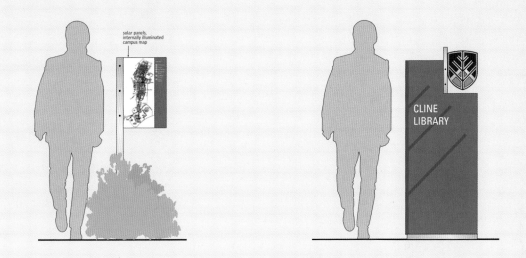

solar panels,
internally illuminated
campus map

CLINE
LIBRARY

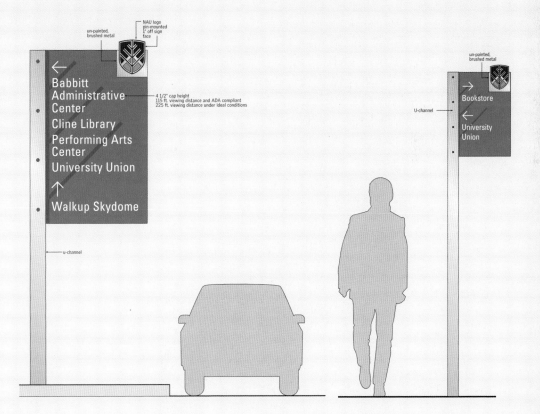

un-painted,
brushed metal

NAU logo
pin-mounted
1" off sign
face

Babbitt
Administrative
Center
Cline Library
Performing Arts
Center
University Union

↑
Walkup Skydome

4 1/2" cap height
115 ft. viewing distance and ADA compliant
225 ft. viewing distance under ideal conditions

u-channel

un-painted,
brushed metal

→ Bookstore

U-channel

← University
Union

HOTEL IDENTITY

the **ZETTER HOTEL**

PROJECT

Zetter Hotel

DESIGNER

Fabian Monheim

CLIENT

Mark Sainsbury & Michael Benyan

I was commissioned to design an identity for a new east London hotel/restaurant called Zetter. The idea was to create a warm place that people could call home, a solid rejection of the cliché of the "design hotel," with its immaculate furniture and maximum space. I wanted do something welcoming and playful, envisioning a common area where the locals could mix with the visitors, bringing a real London feeling into the restaurant.

I began by researching public lettering. The Clerkenwell area has always been London's epicenter for old-style letterpress printing. Fortunately, my long-time studio was a mere five minutes away from the hotel site, so I was already familiar with the neighborhood's various monuments to type—Smithfield Market, St Paul's Cathedral, and so on. I began by finding various fonts that fitted a certain old-fashioned mold. Colorwise, I wanted to restrict the motif of the logo to simple blacks and reds, giving the identity the feel of an old circus poster. Of course, the initial designs altered over time, and the changes produced a mix of the typefaces Clarendon and Shelly, which everyone was happy with.

ABOVE:
Four initial logo sketches and the final logo.

RIGHT:
Assessment of public lettering for inspiration.

FRAKE'S L D. MACE

MEN'S LAVATORY

N⁰ 1
ST. JOHN'S
SQUARE

cheese people

STOP IT STOP IT STOP IT OP IT

GATE 30
MARKET STORES
& WORKSHOPS
SHOP N⁰S
501 - 52

son s ltd

milky

BACK UP
BACK UP

EDMUND MARTIN L

TRIPE DRESSERS. MEAT & OFFAL SALESME
(LINDSEY ST.)

SPRINKLER
STOP VALVE
INSIDE
THE AUTOMATIC SPRINKLER CO LTD

Involving myself in so many different aspects of production was quite a challenge. I'd never worked on a project of this magnitude without a team of producers to back me up. But I've learned that inexperience can add a certain freshness to an overdone topic. I was forced out of my comfort zone, and in order to bring myself closer to a sphere of relevance, I had to unleash a barrage of questions, with the hope that the answers would bring me closer to my subject.

I love designs that stand the test of time. Objects are more valuable if they are not discarded after one viewing. Within two months, most of the ashtrays had been stolen, which I see as the sign of a successful design!

BELOW & FOLLOWING PAGES:
The Zetter identity applied to products and throughout the hotel.

RIGHT:
Poster announcing the opening of Zetter and drawing attention to the hotel's home comforts and innovative services.

The Zetter

Restaurant & Rooms

Victorian **Warehouse** in the heart of **Clerkenwell**

Sandwiched between the City and the West End

7 Rooftop Studios with patios and city views

Opening March 2004

Dramatic five storey Atrium

59 Bedrooms with giant sash windows

Digital Phones with 2 lines and voicemail **Cd-DVD PLAYER** **4000 Track** Digital music library

Flat-screen TV's Movies on demand

Oversized pillows and duvets

Hot water bottles and 2nd hand books

24 hour room service

Modern Italian *Restaurant*

Kitchen open all day **Illustrious wine list**

Weekend brunches

Private dining and no chocolate on your pillow...

PROJECT

Schiller's Liquor Bar

DESIGNER

Matteo Bologna, Mucca Design

CLIENT

Keith McNally

Our work process at Mucca consists of quick thinking and even quicker execution. Mostly, we design book jackets, so we aren't allotted much time. We have to jump right into a project with both feet.

With branding projects, we have more time to devote to the thinking process. We position the brand in its competitive environment, conduct pertinent market research, and browse annuals for inspiring material, particularly those published by the American Institute of Graphic Arts and the Type Directors Club in the USA. When presenting ideas to our clients, we make sure to serve Italian delicacies and plenty of wine. This serves to relax the atmosphere—and besides, the drunker they get, the more inclined they are to look favorably upon our presentation.

Schiller's Liquor Bar

I had a client by the name of Keith McNally who wanted a logo for a new, casual restaurant called Kaminsky's, on the Lower East Side in New York City. It was a typical Jewish name that resided

RIGHT:
Initial sketches for restaurant identity.

Kaminsky's
BAR   RESTAURANT

RESTAURANT

Kaminsky's
BAR

Kaminsky's

Kaminsky's

Bar Kaminsky's

Bar Kaminsky's

comfortably within this neighborhood of Eastern European immigrants. I worked on several versions of the logo, based on old, hand-lettered signs from the 1930s. This was a colossal mistake, because the name of the restaurant soon changed to Alkhool. I was forced to trash my designs and start from scratch. But, before I was able to make yet another transition from paper to computer, the name changed *again*, to Schiller's Liquor Bar. So, weeks passed, and finally one of my designs was chosen. However, before I could heave a sigh of relief, the client decided to go off on an inspirational tour of Europe, returning with a lot of pictures of store signs with the script type that he wanted to use for the logo.

I began the painful process of interpretation, by designing a mono-line script version of the logo that translated into a neon street sign. The client was unhappy with the work, so he hired Nancy Howell, a calligrapher, to design what he had in mind. After she produced several calligraphic pieces, we culled what we needed and modified the logo.

When I create designs for restaurants, I consciously imitate the look of Italian *trattoria* menus, despite the fact that they are the most underdesigned modes of communication I've ever seen. *Trattorias* are mom-and-pop, so while the wife is in the back cooking up a storm, the husband serves the tables in a brusque manner, shoving menus in your face that look like the fiftieth generation Xerox of a Xerox.

BELOW:
Second round of sketches for the renamed restaurant.

RIGHT:
Inspiration provided by the client and third round of sketches.

Schiller's Liquor
Schiller's Bar
Schiller's

Schiller's Liquor Bar

To achieve this look for a modern and organized restaurant in New York City—a revolving-door business, no doubt—I had to create a script face that could be easily updated, yet retained the DIY mentality of these mom-and-pop trattorias. But the problem with script face is that when you have two parallel letters in repetition, you lose the uniqueness of identity that is found in handwriting. I bypassed this problem by creating a typeface with three versions of each glyph. Thanks to Open Type font technology, this made the text look more natural on a menu set down by people who obviously lacked a design portfolio.

Schiller's
LIQUOR BAR

EXHIBITION DESIGN

Quartier Des Spectacles

Intégral Ruedi Baur et Associés

Quartier Des Spectacles Partnership

I don't have a consistent methodology. My work is broad-ranged and interdisciplinary. I work with whomever, with whatever means are at my disposal. My role occurs during the preliminary stages, overseeing the rules of the game, and making sure that the client has accepted the major aspects of a project. Once this is settled, I ease back into the shadows, offering support with helpful whispers, and, in certain key phases like prototyping, reassuming once again a more involved presence.

There are no outstanding methods in the design field; it is a process of continual reinvention. The starting point must remain consistent, for this involves immersion in the minute details of subject matter and the careful analysis of a client's

RIGHT:
Initial sketches for the exhibition.

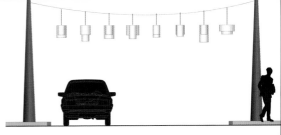

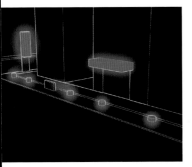
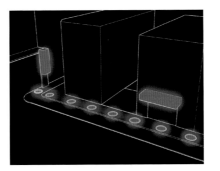
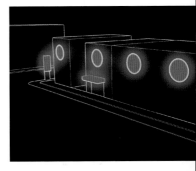

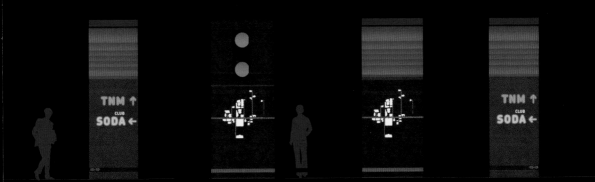

2005

Rapport annuel
du QUARTIER
RUE SAINTE-CATHERINE | MONTRÉAL
DES SPECTACLES

request, but the essence remains in the readdressing of questions, and in questioning the questions, in order to expand the focus and ascertain a potential solution.

The Quartier des Spectacles

This project, initiated in 2002, began as a contest conducted by the architect Jean Beaudoin. The subject was the visual identity of a Montreal neighborhood, which included several dozen cultural venues and 70 percent of Montreal's theater shows. Our goal was to create synergy between the various cultural venues, and, indirectly, yank the neighborhood up by its bootstraps.

We started by giving the neighborhood its own visual language, leaving room for each institution to express itself individually. The chosen theme was the concept of light, a visual language that strengthened the fusion of nightlife and showbiz. The point was not to unify the neighborhood visually, but to create a certain coordination in the presence of various signs. In order to accomplish this, we had to utilize traditional communication media, signage, lighting design, and urban furniture.

MUSEUM EXHIBIT DESIGN

PROJECT

Heta Kuchka Exhibit

DESIGNER

Chris Bolton

CLIENT

Helsinki Museum

When I first start a project, I am overwhelmed at the thought of beginning something new, so I cast it aside for a few hours. As the brief slowly begins to sink in, thoughts creep into my mind. I envision scenarios, shapes, forms, and ideas. The ones that stick are written down without delay. I create endless lists and thoughts, borrowing the imagery of other artists and designers whose work I admire. This process stimulates my mind into figuring out various approaches and ideas. I think it is natural to leapfrog off of other artists. After all, great art is made from what has come before it.

Once I have the foundations of the idea, I sit myself in front of the computer and select colors, forms, and typefaces. It is more a process of seeing what works, of sensing what would be the perfect fit. My job involves injecting new possibilities into stale ideas, to take them beyond what the client originally demonstrated in the brief.

The *idea* is the core of design. Techniques and styles come and go according to the times, but the idea itself is timeless. There are pieces of work out there lacking in ideas, which essentially means that they are soulless.

RIGHT:
Initial sketches for the installation, indicating the positioning of text and images.

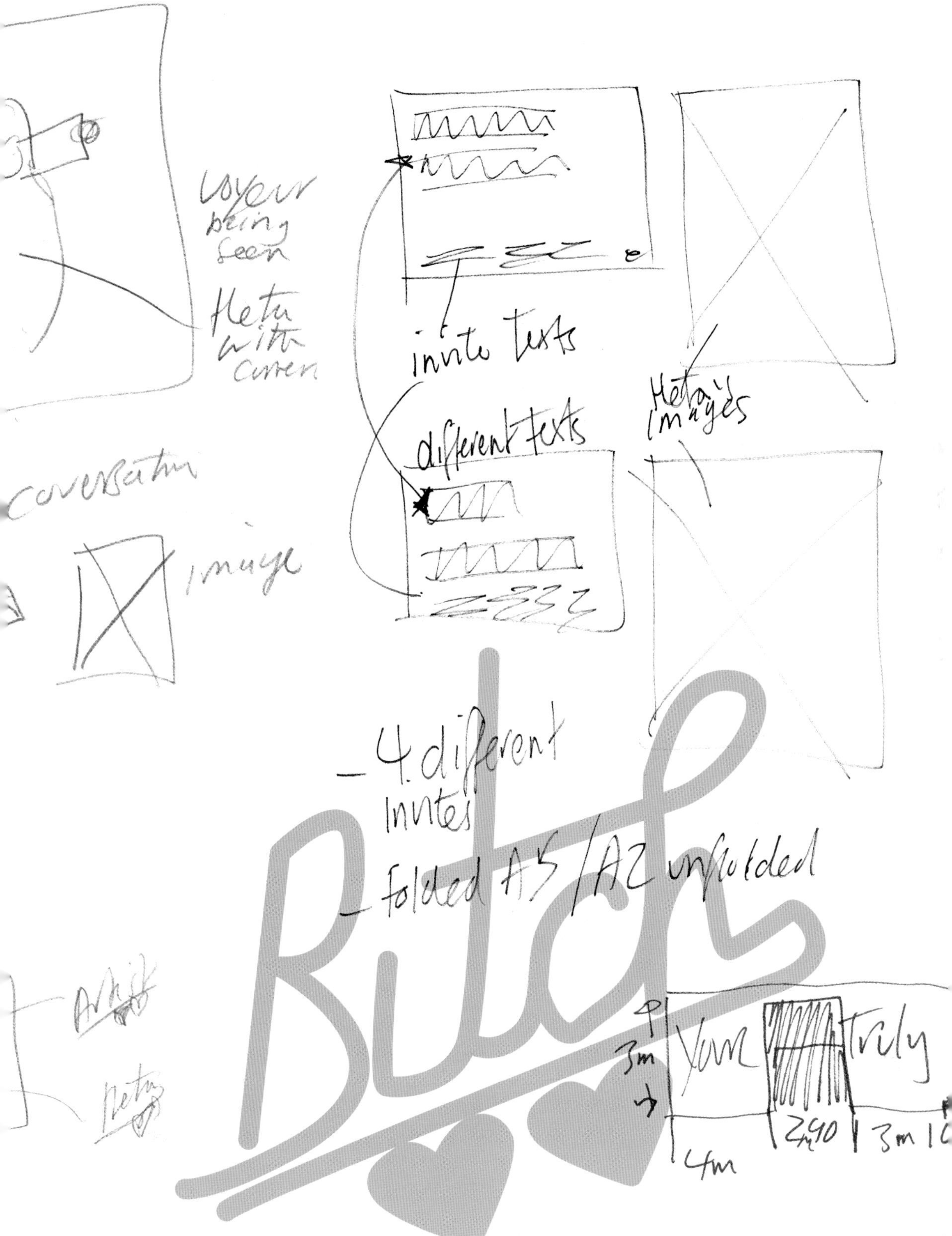

voyeur
being
seen

Hetu
with
Cumen

conversation

[X] image

invite texts

different texts

Hetu's
images

— 4 different
invites
— folded A5 / A2 unfolded

Artist

Hetu

3m

Your   Truly

4m   290   3m 1

SAILORS EVERLASTING LOVE

Taidemuseo Meilahti

Yours Truly Hera Kuchka 6.10. – 10.12.2006
Vuoden nuori taiteilija

Helsingin kaupungin taidemuseolla on ilo kutsua Teidät näytelyn
avajaisiin Meilahteen torstaina 5. lokakuuta 2006 klo 18-20.

Taidemuseo Meilahti
Tamminiementie 6, 00250 Helsinki
Puh. (09) 310 87031
Avoinna ti-su 11-18.30
Lipun 6/3 €, alle 18 v. ilmaiseksi
Pysyväisnäyttelyn ilmainen sisäänpääsy
www.taidemuseo.fi

Årets unga konstnär

Helsingfors stads konstmuseum har nöjet att inbjuda Er till vernissage i
Mejlans torsdagen den 5 oktober 2006 kl. 18-20.

Konstmuseet Mejlans
Elisabethsgatan 6, 00250 Helsingfors
Tel. (09) 310 87031
Öppet ti-sö 11-18.30
Biljetter 6/3 €, under 18 är gratis.
Fritt inträde på fredagar
www.taidemuseo.fi

Young Artist of the Year

Helsinki City Art Museum requests the pleasure of Your company at the
exhibition opening in Meilahti on Thursday, October 5, 2006 at 6-8 p.m.

Art Museum Meilahti
Tamminiementie 6, 00250 Helsinki
Tel. (09) 310 87031
Open Tue-Sun 11am-6.30pm
Admission 6/3 €, under the age of 18 free of charge.
Free admission on fridays
www.taidemuseo.fi

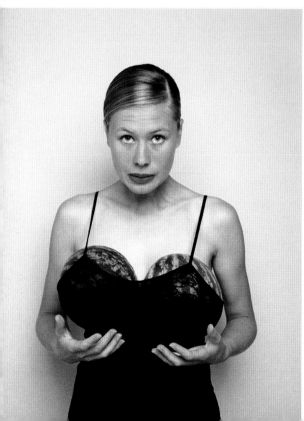

LEFT:
Back of invitation poster.

ABOVE:
Heta Kuchka's work used on
the front of invitation posters.

It is true that graphic design is hard work, but it is also enjoyable. When I am feeling stressed, I remind myself that I am getting paid to do something that I take true pleasure in, while other people in the world have to work awful jobs just to pay the bills. I am lucky to have this amazing opportunity.

I worked alongside Heta in a Helsinki exhibition held in her honor. This was a great opportunity to create something new that could be incorporated into her work. Previously, the exhibition had been named Yours Truly, but we wanted to revamp it so we tossed around some new ideas. I wanted to call it Bitch!—a title I felt bridged all of her work—but in the end we kept the original.

We set out creating ideas for the invitation, referencing past exhibitions, even as we gradually distanced ourselves. Heta's style is photographic, documentary-like, and text-based, so we used this in the relating materials.

The typographic anagrammatic title was derived from the titles of Heta's artwork. Since I worked closely with her on this project and a book, I was familiar with her accomplishments.

The original titles are as follows:

- Sailors
- Life goes on
- What if...
- For better or worse
- Sweethearts
- Kiss

Together, we formed anagrams and installed related imagery. We had other options, but these fitted so well and were mildly amusing, so we were satisfied.

I'm not sure why we used the English titles and not the Finnish. Perhaps it trickled down from the main exhibition's title, and took off from there. Heta sprang from an American/Finnish background, so perhaps that informed the decision.

RIGHT:
Floor installation.
Outdoor signage.
Wall installation.

CONFERENCE BRANDING

VM World Conference 2007

Brian Rea & Nicholas Blechman

VM World Conference

Nicholas Blechman and I worked on a project with Todd Richards at Cahan & Associates in San Francisco that consisted of 30 line-art illustrations, created in order to help brand the VM World 2007 conference held in the Moscone Center. Part of the branding involved massive banners and signage, including one huge wall facing the entrance of the convention center. Todd had seen the Ideas issue for *The New York Times Magazine* that Christoph Niemann, Nicholas Blechman, and I had worked on with Kristina DiMatteo, and he thought it might be cool to have us create a chalkboard illustration in front of a live audience. This was a terrifying prospect, as there were going to be something like 11,000 attendees, but we jumped at the opportunity nevertheless, for as illustrators and designers, we rarely get to interact with so large an audience. It proved to be a terrific experience. While we were working, people would saunter over and talk to us, offer suggestions,

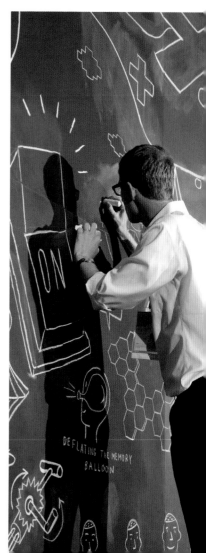

or simply stand and watch. The whole process made us look at what we were doing in an entirely different light—work so often done in private suddenly made so nakedly public—and this taught us about the limitations of our form, and how far we could truly push the boundaries.

The project took four days, with one-hour lunch breaks and endless cups of coffee. The hardest part was the great wall, which turned out to be 60ft wide x 16ft tall (approx 18m x 5m), making this into a mammoth undertaking. It forced us into the realization that this was an installation as opposed to the drawing exercises we had in mind—we'd already done a series of sketches based on 200 "tech terms" that Todd had sent us. The conference attendees were naturally conversant with the lingo, though Nicholas and I had very little knowledge of the meaning of word pairings such as "hyper-visor." Our lack of expertise was an advantage, though, since it allowed us to reinvent the meanings in our line drawings, and we compiled the 300 ideas we had come up with into one large sketch that would fit the entire wall. In the end, Cahan had to rent a scissor lift and hire a security guard round the clock to keep an eye on everything. We brought in Doug, a local union guy, to help us out, and for four days he raised and lowered the scissor lift. By the end, we'd enlisted him to do some drawing, and he turned out to be pretty good with lettering.

We met at the wall at 9 a.m. and drew all day, calling it quits by 5 p.m. Many decisions had to be made along the way concerning chalk thickness, scale, and hierarchy, since the sketches we were working from were 2in (5cm) tall and the canvas we were using was mountainous in comparison. We followed the sketches as best we could, reworking larger ideas into smaller ones, and filling things in along the way. There was plenty of room for improvisation and free-styling, though these were always couched on the specific "tech terms" given us. What we'd gleaned from the slips of paper left in the suggestion box in the convention hall helped us formulate and sharpen our ideas, and being able to erase and redraw whenever we needed to was a big help, too.

I had hoped that Christoph would join us, but since his wife was expecting a baby at the time, this was not possible. Still, working

with Nicholas again was amazing—he is a raging machine of ideas and dedication. It is really inspiring to watch him work, for his energy would transmit to me and we'd parry possibilities and ideas back and forth with the alacrity and energy of a ball in an intense ping-pong match. We'd worked together before, so there is a tremendous amount of respect and trust between us, which made this a great collaboration.

After the conference, the wall was dismantled piece by piece, and sprayed with dead-flat varnish. It is now installed at VM Ware's corporate campus office in Palo Alto, California.

LEFT:
Brian and Nicholas in front of the Great Wall. The wall consisted of 30 4ft x 8ft (1.2m x 2.4m) panels.

The finished product.

FOLLOWING PAGES:
Detail of the first third of the wall.

MERCHANDISE DESIGN

PROJECT

Snoopy in Japan

DESIGNER

Fabian Monheim

CLIENT

we've

The Snoopy project began as a commission to design a fragrance for the beloved character created by Charles Schulz. This involved the packaging, naming, graphics, and the creation of an actual scent. I thought this was a wonderfully strange project, though I had no idea why they chose me, a notorious chainsmoker who hadn't worn cologne in years.

Once I was back in Japan, I began by imagining what Snoopy would smell like. I envisioned security blankets, pumpkins, fresh laundry, and baking cookies. I saw Snoopy lying on top of his house, looking up at the stars. I searched for layers of Snoopy memory and sensed fun, fruity, and friendly design possibilities. I discovered that Snoopy's sister was called Belle, so my very first name proposal was Belle 55 & Eau de Snoopy, or Snoopium, which later merged into Snoopy 55.

After countless meetings with representatives from the Japanese Institute of Perfume, where we sampled and worked to refine the fragrance, we gave birth to the first Snoopy perfume. When I proposed the packaging graphics, the clients were bowled over by the style and commissioned me to do all the graphics and merchandising for the exhibition. Snoopy was an easy subject for

ABOVE:
Snoopy fragrance packaging.

RIGHT:
Snoopy graphic from fragrance packaging used for the Snoopy 55th Anniversary exhibit.

The Essential Principles of Graphic Design

me, since I was a huge fan of the *Peanuts* gang. The characters always struck me as being far more real than their cartoon personas, with a universal appeal that spanned many generations. A child could relate to the absolute cuteness of the characters and their situations, and adults could empathize with the depression and misery of Charlie Brown. I created a brief, focusing on a more contemporary look, though I was careful not to detract from Snoopy's iconic status. I reduced him to a silhouette, making it much easier to use his figure in patterns or as a graphic element, and this added a certain fashionable flair to the exhibition.

The material for the exhibition was provided by numerous Tokyo artists and designers, who interpreted their vision of Snoopy's life.

LEFT:
Snoopy icons.

BELOW:
Cookie packaging.

SNOOPY
Heartful Stay*
PEANUT BALL COOKIES

IMPERIAL HOTEL
TOKYO

Happiness is
THE 55th
ANNIVERSARY

アトリエワン
アリタマサフミ
宇津木えり
草間彌生
クラインダイサム・アーキテクツ
倉科昌高
シアター・プロダクツ
生意気
坂茂
深澤直人
伏見京子
村山留里子
森本千絵
池内タオル
エイベックス・鈴木亜美
かまわぬ
熊崎俊太郎
黒田泰蔵
スティーブン・ジョーンズ
杉野宣雄
鈴懸
テオブロマ
トリンプ
バカラ
ニコライ バーグマン
ファビアン・モンハイム
藤野征一郎
三浦加納子
三谷龍二
美濃和紙ネットワーク21
森正洋
吉川真由
4℃
D-BROS（グラフィックデザイン）
みかんぐみ（エキシビションデザイン）

東京国際フォーラム　ホールA
2005年11月19日〜2006年1月15日　※会期中無休
11:00〜19:30（最終入場は19:00まで）大人1300円、中学生800円、小学生500円

2005 11/19 SAT
- 2006 1/15 SUN

Organizer:　産経新聞社／テレビ東京／スヌーピーライフデザイン展製作委員会　　Supporter:　テレビ東京ブロードバンド／ディノス／東京メトロ
Collaborator:　ユナイテッド・メディア／ティターミンドプロダクションズ／スヌーピータウンショップ／図書印刷　Venue Constructor: ㈱乃村工藝社
Sponsor:　トヨタ／サークルKサンクス／UFJカード／ANA全日空

LEFT:
Snoopy 55th anniversary poster.

ABOVE:
Photos from the exhibition.

WINDOW DISPLAY DESIGN

PROJECT

Power Flower

DESIGNER

Antenna Design

CLIENT

Bloomingdale's New York

We never follow a standard operating procedure, since the majority of our projects are vastly different from each other. Still, there are some commonalities in terms of approach. We start by setting off on "learning missions." This includes tapping into client knowledge, going on field trips, making casual observations, reading, and astute note-taking. Questions are posed. Who is the client? Who is the audience? Where is this going and what will it do? This allows us to frame the project appropriately. Carefully, like a predator observing prey, we scope out the context—sniffing out the subject, reading the terrain—before we pounce.

Power Flower, which we remember quite fondly, was not a typical design program. In 2001, a few months after the terrorist attacks of 9/11, Häagen-Dazs decided to initiate a cultural marketing campaign. They invited us to create a proposal, which was to be displayed in the Lexington Avenue windows of Bloomingdale's flagship store. We were to build a design based around the theme of "buoying spirits," which New Yorkers sorely needed at the time. We tossed around countless ideas, keeping in mind that the design's

ABOVE:
Sketch for laser-projected
window display.

appeal needed to be universal, and we finally settled on one: laser-projected flowers that bloomed with each pedestrian's passing. The message was simple, for flowers are a symbol of life and beauty, and the energy emanating from New Yorkers can make beautiful things happen.

Here's what we did. We ordered cheap "home disco" laser projectors and took them apart—we figured we'd be able to hack something together when the time came. Then we made illustrations and an interactive diagram that communicated the idea, and sent it off. Everyone loved it and we were hired. That was the easy part—the brain-freeze was shortly to follow.

We needed to figure out how to make the installation work. Realizing that we needed more space for projection, which would require larger instruments and a city permit, it turned out that the laser approach was not feasible after all. So we had to come up with another way to realize the original concept, and quickly. A glimpse into other technologies led to an LED solution. However, we needed 40,000 blue LEDs. There wasn't a place in the US that had enough of them in stock, and nobody overseas could guarantee that our order would arrive in time. We'd reached a low point.

But then we hit upon the idea of making flowers out of neon lighting. To our surprise, we learned that making custom neon lights was both fast and inexpensive and, overall, would work much better since neon has a physical presence in the darkness.

When we went back to Häagen-Dazs and said that the project had morphed into neon, they were not thrilled. Neon lights held a negative connotation as far as they were concerned, and it took some skillful persuasion to convince them that neon was far and away the best choice. After winning them over, we worked at mach-speed, regretfully lacking the time needed to experiment with the electronics and to test the system logistics. It was a real daredevil approach—we were forced to address issues whenever they surfaced. Even as a gawking crowd began to gather outside the window, we were still scrambling to make last-minute adjustments. The project ran for three weeks in January of 2002, and we still receive compliments to this day, making it all worthwhile.

ABOVE:
New sketch for neon light window display.

RIGHT:
Final window design.

PROJECT

New York Metropolitan Opera Website

DESIGNER

Hillman Curtis

CLIENT

New York Metropolitan Opera

When working on the web I am concerned with designing systems that reveal their beauty through simplicity and functionality. Part of the process concerns the discovery of a touchstone—usually a word or phrase—that defines the core of the project. I find that it is useful to refer to the touchstones to ensure the integrity of the design.

I rarely use wireframes. If the client has someone on their team who has them, that is fine, but I want to see the type, layout, and color almost immediately. I absolutely hate showing wireframes as part of a review. The argument in bigger corporations is that if you show the vice president the design work, as opposed to wireframes, they'll focus on the color and not on the functionality—which is wrong. I want the client to be involved with the design at every level. I start with a subpage, usually a form page or registration path, and this back-door

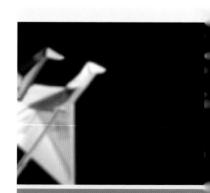

rfly

o6

Sunday, Decemb

- 12 Noon
- 1:00 PM
- 3:00 PM
- 8:00 PM
- 8:00 PM

Monday, Decemt

- 10AM – 8PM
- 12:30 PM
- 6:00 PM
- 6:15 PM
- 8:00 PM

approach allows me to find the design through function-centric pages. This way the client isn't as anxious as they normally would be when we're working on the homepage. We sneak up on them. Recently, I was brought in to do some next-generation concepts for a major online property. This is a client with whom I'd had a successful relationship for the last three years. The team I normally worked with was involved in a beta launch and had very little time to give me, which was a problem. My process is collaborative, and I simply couldn't generate substantive concepts on my own. I should have suggested that the project be placed on hold, but instead I ended up pounding my head against the wall for a week, and coughed up a few paltry concepts. I'm not sure I recovered from that one.

The New York Metropolitan Opera website

Pentagram's Paula Scher recommended me for the Metropolitan Opera site redesign. Paula did their rebranding, so before I met with Peter Gelb, the new director of the Metropolitan Opera, I stopped at Pentagram to talk with Paula about her experience. She showed me her work—the new logotype was simple yet elegant, done in 10-point Baskerville with subtle shadings of gray and white. I asked her what I should focus on in the site redesign, and she pointed to the white space surrounding the logotype in her comprehensive designs. She explained that the logotype would be compromised if it were crowded, for the whole point was to communicate a sense of openness, the Metropolitan Opera's new theme.

Peter Gelb echoed this theme when he shared his hopes for the Metropolitan Opera. He explained that opera was seen as an art form for the upper classes, and he wanted to shed this perception and create a new one, which would show it as the rich, vibrant, and democratic art form it has long sought to become, open to one and all. Making action of his ideology, Peter planned free events, open houses, and tours. He opened a gallery in the building and hosted contemporary artists in a variety of media. He opened a small theater devoted to screenings of operas and, unsurprisingly, displayed interest in many forms of media on the Opera's website,

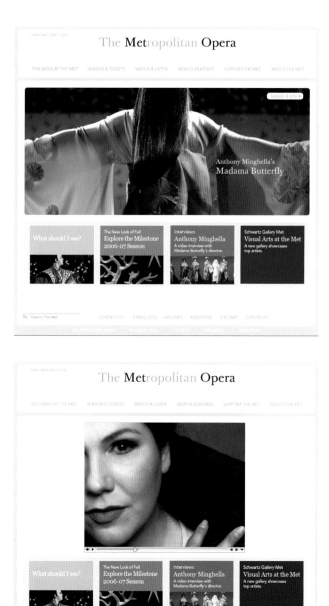

including video, audio, chats, and blogs. He wanted the Opera to be seen as a beehive of creative energy with an open-door policy, and, in order to do this, he understood the importance of tapping into various media.

The first step in my design process involves meeting the members of the client's team—in the corporate world, these people are referred to as "stakeholders." I often ask for a full day of their time, and in the case of the Metropolitan Opera, I received two half-days in a conference room in their building. This was all the time I needed to work through the goals of the redesign.

I asked Noreen Morioka, of AdamsMorioka, to join me. At the time, I was working solo out of a home office in San Francisco, so Noreen offered support with the complex task of managing and aiding the design of the project. We began by identifying the foremost goal of the site—usually, this has something to do with commerce, paired with something less concrete—and we decide to continue the "openness" theme.

Having this theme in mind helped me make some basic design decisions. The site would have a white or light-colored background, and simplicity would inform every page. But I wasn't able to begin the design until I engaged in the time-consuming task of reorganizing the site map, as well as determining the major templates I needed. Most large sites have a content management system and some sort of back-end database, which have to be considered prior to design. After a day or two of labor, we had a decent site map, a list of templates, and a fair understanding of the back-end technology.

I designed the header and navigation first. I had Paula's rebrand style guide close at hand during this phase, knowing full well that the header would house the logotype. My first inclination was to float it above the page without structure or housing, but this looked terrible and incomplete. I knew that I needed to establish a consistent, weighted presence, one that drew the user's eye not only to the logo but also to the navigation and login greeting. I opted for a curved framework that kept things soft and open.

PREVIOUS PAGES:
Details from the New York
Metropolitan Opera website.

LEFT:
Grid and system for the website.

Examples of different homepages.

The **Met**ropolitan **Opera**

THIS WEEK AT THE MET   SEASON & TICKETS   WATCH & LISTEN   NEWS & FEATURES   SUPPORT THE MET   ABOUT THE MET

Madama Butterfly
Tonight!

Composer: Giacomo Puccini
Librettists: Giuseppe Giacosa, Luigi Illica
Sung in Italian with Met Titles in English

September 25, – November 18, 2006

 tickets & info ▸

SEASON CALENDAR

December 2006   View Full Calendar

S	M	T	W	T	F	S
26	27	28	29	30	1	2
3	4	5	6	7	8	9
10	11	12	13	14	15	16
17	18	19	20	21	22	23
24	25	26	27	28	29	30
31	1	2	3	4	5	6

What Should I See?

The Arnold and Marie Schwartz Gallery Met Exhibit
Richard Prince

Live Online
Mazeppa

Sunday, December 10, 2006   NEXT WEEK ▸

- **12 Noon** — New painting unveiled in The Arnold and Marie Schwartz Gallery
- **1:00 PM** — Sunday Met series: XYZ (List Hall)
- **3:00 PM** — National Council Finals
- **8:00 PM** — Streaming of 1990 performance of FGH (on this site)
- **8:00 PM** — Aretha Franklin performance

Monday, December 11, 2006

- **10AM – 8PM** — The Arnold and Marie Schwartz Gallery Met exhibit
- **12:30 PM** — Anna Netrebko Signing (Opera Shop)
- **6:00 PM** — Patron Cocktail Reception in The Arnold and Marie Schwartz Gallery
- **6:15 PM** — Master Class with Joan Dornemann (Kaplan Penthouse)
- **8:00 PM** — MAZEPPA performance (Streamed on this site)

Tuesday, December 12, 2006

- **10AM – 8PM** — The Arnold and Marie Schwartz Gallery Met exhibit
- **5:00 PM** — Book Signing (Opera Shop)
- **6:00 PM** — Lecture: Verdi's Father-Daughter Duets (Kaplan Penthouse)
- **8:00 PM** — LA FORZA DEL DESTINO performance (Streamed on this site)

Wednesday, December 13, 2006

- **10AM – 8PM** — The Arnold and Marie Schwartz Gallery Met exhibit
- **10AM – 6PM** — Open House in front lobby spaces, for tickets call xxx
- **2:00 PM** — Master Class with xyz (Kaplan Penthouse)
- **5:00 PM** — Live Green Room Chat with Natalie Dessay
- **8:00 PM** — CYRANO DE BERGERAC performance (Streamed on this site)

Saturday, December 16, 2006

- **10AM – 8PM** — The Arnold and Marie Schwartz Gallery Met exhibit
- **1:30PM** — Radio Broadcast of LA FORZA DEL DESTINO
- **2:00PM** — LA FORZA DEL DESTINO performance (Streamed on this site)
- **8:00PM** — CYRANO DE BERGERAC performance
- **8:00PM** — Streaming of 1990 performance of XYZ on this site

I begin my designs with a 10px (gutter) by 40px (box) grid. I used this same grid in the early stages of a Yahoo homepage redesign, the My Yahoo! page concepts, the Adobe.com redesign, and many others. I eventually abandoned it in favor of a 5px by 5px grid.

I start with a subpage—never on the homepage or landing page. This allows me to make many small design decisions that will later influence the major landing-page design. It is also relatively pressure-free, unlike the homepage. For the Metropolitan Opera, we started on the director's biography page, which allowed us to come up with sub- and side-navigation, text styles, leading, color, and click and hover states for links.

There was some pressure from the Opera to see a homepage comprehensive. One of the disadvantages of starting with a subpage is that you get so engrossed with following the directives set by the page that you forget that the homepage and landing pages need more punch. My comprehensives for the homepage were so dull that I turned to Sean Adams for help. I sent him an almost complete page with photos and a solid layout, though there was definitely a missing element. Sean took the bottom four feature buckets, covered the photos halfway with a block of color, cleaned up the type treatments, and transformed what I had done into a beautiful, color-filled page.

The homepage had to be adaptable; it needed to accommodate multiple media. The large size of the feature area of the page was made to measure, in order to fit the display of rich imagery and the sizable video player.

This was matter of applying the system—the combination of functionality developed through the subpages, and the color and type developed on the home page—across the site.

PERSONAL BLOG DESIGN

PROJECT

Subtraction.com

DESIGNER

Khoi Vinh

CLIENT

Self-Published

When starting a project, before I do anything else, I sketch in an informal manner. The point of this method is to quickly get ideas onto paper, discard them, and generate new ones at a continually rapid pace. I don't worry about implementation or execution at all. I belong to that school which deems sketching as an informal process, as a means of generating ideas—not to be confused with documents created for posterity. I need to feel completely uninhibited when I sketch, which is why I use random sheets of paper that can be torn up, scissored, or tossed away without compunction. I always carry a Moleskine notebook around the city with me, a handy tool for personal, impromptu doodling.

My next step involves creating a grid. I will often go back and sketch if the grid and the preliminary blocking out of elements don't successfully translate my original ideas. In the past, I've used Adobe Illustrator, but in recent years I've favored working in Adobe Photoshop. I'll use this to render the high-fidelity mock-ups that serve as the last stage before coding. Personally, I prefer not to jump immediately into code until I've come to a very specific conclusion as to how it should be rendered. This enables me to work on the ideas of the design with a certain speed before I begin to handle the execution.

ABOVE:
Examples of Khoi Vihn's work displayed in the portfolio section of Subtraction.com.

Depending on whether or not I'm working solo, I'll then code the pages manually, or turn the Photoshop comprehensives over to a design technologist, who will also take a hands-on approach. I never use a WYSIWYG application like Dreamweaver. It may have evolved in the decade or so since I last tried it, but it always made me feel as if I was doing needlepoint with mittens on.

Subtraction, version 1

I'd never built such a complex site before, so for me it was the ideal way to learn about my medium. I went about this with all the bustle and ambition of a major corporation, although I was a moonlighting force of one. I was focused on a transparent yet complicated hierarchy: make the organization intelligible yet deeply layered, and display content on the grid so that information can easily be found. I was trying my best to remain true to the medium. I used a lot of graphical text (e.g. text typeset in gifs or jpegs), but the bulk was coded in HTML and rendered by the browser.

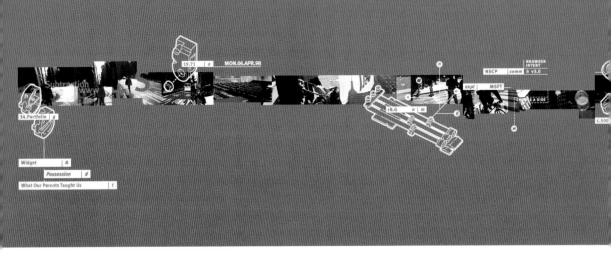

Subtraction, version 3

Here I created a much simpler and flatter hierarchy: working
abstractly, I merely added things to the right at random. I figured
that there would be no explicit logic to the left-to-right organization,
so I filled it with things that interested me: digital shots of street
scenes, diagrams of useless machine parts that I'd drawn, and
nonsensical diagrammatic call-outs and notations. The whole
thing was reflective of what print designers like myself seek
to create as soon as we began to feel comfortable on the web:
obfuscated information.

ABOVE:
Subtraction.com, version 3.

RIGHT:
Subtraction.com, version 4.

Subtraction, version 4

I dialed back from the abstract approach and tried to split the
difference with version 1. Once again, the hierarchy is flat. The
idea was to add new stuff to the top and push the older stuff to
the bottom. This was very much like a blog, in fact, but executed
without the benefit of blogging software.

Subtraction, version 7

I learned more about web-standard mark-up and coding in
a semantically correct way by remaining true to the medium.
I combined everything I'd learned on the organization of
information—the newest-at-the-top postings, the left-to-right
hierarchy, emphasizing HTML text over graphical text—and

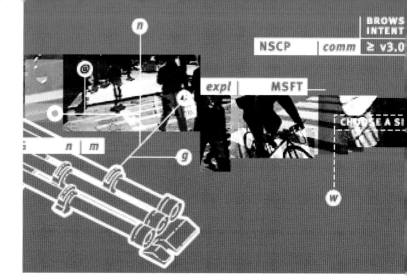

n

expl | MSFT

g

i | n | m

w

CHOOSE A SI

Subtraction

+S

version 4.0

Subtraction | 4.0b2   **Nineteen Hundred and Ninety Nine**

Optimized for version 4.x+ browsers.

Made with Macintosh.

03.02.99 What Our Parents Taught Us | Number 3: Percent Happy

+ Third in a series of ten image explorations.

This is a high bandwidth image at ± 330 k.

02.10.99 siteGrease Announced

+ siteGrease is a FileMaker Pro database that allows users to store log-on names and passwords. Released as freeware, with full access to all layouts and scripts.

02.07.99 What Our Parents Taught Us | Number 1: Guard Dogs & Children

+ A table structure in the consumer domain, relocalized. First in a series of ten image explorations.

This is a high bandwidth image at ± 151 k.

02.07.99 What Our Parents Taught Us | Number 2: Telephony

+ A table structure in the consumer domain, relocalized. Second in a series of ten image explorations.

This is a high bandwidth image at ± 262 k.

02.06.99 Subtraction Version 4.0b1 Beta Launch

+ Beta debut for the latest iteration of Subtraction, featuring a redesigned UI, collapsed and simplified site architecture, and revised content scope.

This site is currently in beta. Please send feedback and comments.

hammered my design flag into the ground as I refined my online voice. I struggled in comprehensives for a while because I wanted to make a very bold statement. Finally, I hit upon the idea of draining all the color away and creating a black-and-white presentation. I was pretty nervous, since the few people who saw the project before it was launched didn't care for it, but I was confident what I had made was representative of the type of work I wanted to do, so I went with my instinct and found myself pleased by the results.

After working in the field for so long, and armed with the experience and honing of my craft that only time and energy can bring, I've come to realize what makes design great. In its contexts, both of an immediate and larger scale, we find what informs it. But in order to tap into the greatness of the form, questions must be posed. Does it work for the audience? What role does it play in business? What are the constraints that inform it? Quite a few times I've made the mistake of thinking that I could create great designs for projects and clients I didn't believe in. I've worked with uncomfortable idioms I thought were going to be easy to manage—consumer goods and fashion spring to mind—but my confidence and idealism have often betrayed me. Ultimately, the work produced was less than satisfactory. It is true that a great designer can design anything, but no designer can create brilliantly unless the work is challenging enough to match his or her boundless passion.

Subtraction

Version 7.0
Khoi Vinh's Web Site

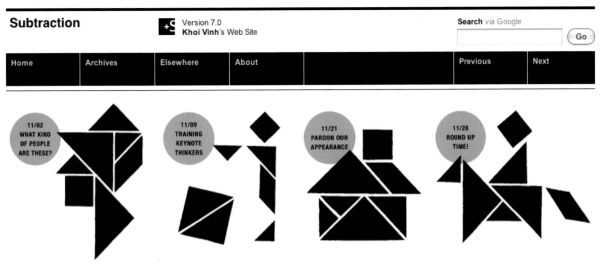

| 11/02 WHAT KIND OF PEOPLE ARE THESE? | 11/09 TRAINING KEYNOTE THINKERS | 11/21 PARDON OUR APPEARANCE | 11/28 ROUND UP TIME! |

November 2006

10 posts

	Sunday	Monday	Tuesday	Wednesday	Thursday	Friday	Saturday
				01	02	03	04
	05	06	07	08	09	10	11
	12	13	14	15	16	17	18
	19	20	21	22	23	24	25
	26	27	28	29	30		

November's illustration was created by **Rob Giampietro**, of the design studio Giampietro + Smith. To see the studio's work, visit **studio-gs.com**. More of Rob's own writing on design can be found at **lineandunlined.com**.

Wed 29 Nov 2006

All Feeded Up

08:49 PM
REMARKS (31)

Here's a confession: I'm a *terrible* blog friend.

Over the past few years, I've been fortunate enough to have met scores of really interesting people thanks to my work with **my old company**, my new position at **NYTimes.com**, and **Subtraction.com** — people inside and outside of these companies,

Quick Access

1196 posts since July 2000.

Date	Select...	
Categories	Select...	

PROJECT

Four Community Websites

DESIGNER

Armin Vit & Bryony Gomez-Palacio

CLIENT

Under Consideration, LLC

Armin:

I divide a project's trajectory into three phases: research, design, and wrap-up. Research is the most important phase—I am able to design faster, and with greater accuracy, when I gather relevant information. I try to stay on top of what is going on in sports, culture, and business in order to make timely references. It is also the perfect excuse to roam the internet endlessly, watch *The Simpsons*, and read *Entertainment Weekly*.

Research usually takes from a week to a month, depending upon the project. Once the information is in place, I let it simmer. I often design in my head, away from the computer, without a sketchbook or pen at hand. I'm not very good at sketching. For me, a blank file

ABOVE:
Logo sketches.

Old logo for Speak Up.

typography, and random crops of images or illustrations. I miss having my sketches, and I miss referencing half-cooked ideas, yet there is something incredibly rewarding in sitting myself down in front of the computer and seeing something so cohesive formulate on the screen.

Once I arrive at an idea that has potential, I obsess about how every element should come together. Nothing is arbitrary. I work a lot in picas, and usually everything is divisible by Op3, in one form or another. This may not make for perfect design, but it helps me cope with the organization of any layout, granting me a profound pleasure when everything is justified. Symmetry is poetry in still life.

I am struck by the realization that everything we design could be constructed in a hundred different ways; what matters most is the rationalization you put behind the work. Also integral to the process is the agreement made between you and the client as to the appropriateness of the design, for without the client, there is no project. Designers can argue all the day long over point size, colors, and paper with clients until they get their way, but if the idea itself is strong enough, it doesn't matter if it's blue, red, or in 12-point type.

When I like a design, or am as happy with it as I could possibly get, I am ready to enter the presentation stage. This is where the real fun begins, listening to client feedback and finding ways to meet their demands while bearing in mind your own intentions. This is the point in the journey where I find myself at the crossroads between commerce and compromise. Until the finalization of the project, there's a lot of obsessing about having a clean file and making sure nothing falls out of place. Fortunately, the end of the process is rewarded with more internet browsing.

Bryony:

Graphic design is always full of surprises. No matter how many times you say, "Been there, done that," you're always forced to reevaluate. Each project and each client is unique. You explore new ideas and new subjects, combing over the mysterious terrain. There's so much ground to cover that it's dizzying to realize how

the design encyclopedia

ABOVE:
Final logos.

New Speak Up logo.

much is truly unmapped. Of course, nothing is perfect. As there's always room for improvement, there will also be just enough room for errors to slip in. My mistakes usually stem from lack of sleep. This leads to distraction, a foregoing of details that could land me in the cannibal soup: typos, a missed change, missing supporting files, or an important phone call, writing incomplete specs, and a host of other minor disasters. Individually, the mistakes are miniscule, but when they tend to accumulate in one week, or in one particular project, you sink deeper and faster into the sludge. The best thing to do is to shut down the computer, take a long nap, and restart with a gigantic cup of coffee and an updated calendar.

RIGHT:

Speakup.com, October 2002.

Speakup.com, November 2007.

Speak Up

Speak Up was born in 2001, but not as a blog. It wasn't until 2002, with the advent of MovableType, a blog publishing system, that Speak Up took off as a design discussion site. The basic look and feel of the site has remained steadfast from its genesis to the present. We've never removed ourselves from the three-column approach, or the basic layout of the sidebars. The changes we've made over the years have been, for the most part, with the intention of making the content quick and easy to browse. We also introduced elements such as Word It, and created space for advertising.

In 2006 we were forced into a redesign because our database crashed. Whereas before it was composed of all rows and labels, we tried a different approach and wound up doing a CSS-driven layout, making all the colors brighter. One of the biggest changes, however, has been the logo. It began as this quirky, semi-pixelated emoticon with a weird speech bubble, based on the speech depictions in pre-Hispanic Mexican drawings. In 2004, I asked calligrapher Michael Clark to design a new logo.

Concerning UnderConsideration, the change has been more drastic. It began as a landing page for the unfortunates who honed in on the main URL, looking for Speak Up. At the time, we weren't sure what UnderConsideration was supposed to be. When we launched *The Design Encyclopedia*, we altered the design to make it appear more official. It helped that we had some news to share now and then, so we were able to populate that right column semi-regularly.

Speak Up

A DIVISION OF UNDER CONSIDERATION

AUTHORS · ABOUT · CONTACT

SPEAK UP

version 2.1 · bigger, badder, gentler · just for you

01-05 | 06-10 | 11-15

So what exactly is this place? ★ comments ★

what's the deal with the logo? ★ comments ★

let me go please ★ comments ★

convergence ★ comments ★

first speak up ★ comments ★

contributors to this space

PERSON IN CHARGE
- ARMIN VIT
- TONI COX
- BRYONY GOMEZ-PALACIO
- ANTONIO GOMEZ-PALACIO
- RICK VALICENTI
- RYAN ZDENKA

ENTRY COUNT: 13
LAST UPDATED: 09.19.02

Should you like to contribute just click here

HELP WANTED! Immediate Opening. Part-time. Authors to push ideas and findings. Open mind is a must. Design knowledge preferred. Excellent benefits. Applicant must be energetic, creative and motivated. If interested, please click here!

DESIGN DEALS

This topic was already covered in Typographica a few months back. I know because I started the heated discussion. But I want to see what happens when the same "problem" is posed to designers, rather than the typographer crowd that hangs around Typographica. Not that there is anything wrong with that.

What am I talking about? Logos done for as cheap as $0.99, and if you hit the right price you can even get a happy meal. Do these companies hurt the Design profession? Is it just too cheap? does it fill a niche?

And what about this designer in a box? I always kid around on how if you press Shift-F3 on a computer a logo comes out. But this software does just that with prefabricated templates. This program even boasts your client's niche who draws really good and can do the logo for free.

I stated it once, and I'll say it again, **I think it hurts the design profession.** Does it fill a need in the market? Definitely. Do I like it? No.

You get what you pay for.

POSTED BY **ARMIN** on 10.03.2002 | COMMENTS [7]

IT'S A WIDE WORLD AFTER ALL

It's time for some international flavor. Being from Mexico, I'll talk about that country and let any other foreigners talk about their respective countries.

Design in Mexico is not viewed as a great career path to follow, some people get a Bachelor's degree in Design because it's an easy four year program, others join because they can draw pretty pictures. And even sadder than that, a woman attending college for a Design degree is assumed to be there just killing time while she finds a suiting husband.

The good thing is that there are other people that really like design and understand what it's all about. There are some great design firms and organizations. The biggest break we've had so far, for recognition, is a feature article in Communication Arts "VIVA DISEÑO" A very well written and researched article that truly conveys the design scene in Mexico.

One day I'll go back and hope to be part of the design community that is slowly, but strongly, building there. Here are some design firms: (It's hard to find web sites, not everybody is as web happy as the US or Europe):

- GABRIEL MARTINEZ MRAVE
- HULA-HULA
- PABLO MEYER (don't get scared by the ugly site, it gets better)

POSTED BY **ARMIN** on 10.02.2002 | COMMENTS [9]

MARTHA KNOWS TYPE

My wife subscribes to Martha Stewart Living and every now and then I'll pick it up just to see what's inside. First time I flipped through I thought it was a pretty well designed magazine. By now I have developed a liking for Martha Stewart Living. This morning as I was having breakfast I skimmed through the latest issue (October 2002) where they are showing off their new redesign, starting with a **very** nice custom typeface family that really shines in the new layout. Remember, we are talking design, not content. The photographs are always great and very well shot. The layout is clean, the headers are big and brightly colored and the slight rareness by Trade Gothic round it out to be a great publication. I recommend that you take a quick peek at it, don't be ashamed, it's not as bad as picking up an adult magazine at Borders. Plus, where else can you find out how to stop squirrels from eating your light bulbs?

If anybody has any information on the typeface please let us know. It is one of the best typefaces I have seen in a long time. And people say there is nothing left to explore in typeface design.

*Update: I have scanned a few samples of the type as requested.

POSTED BY **ARMIN** on 09.26.2002 | COMMENTS [13]

COVERED

For any avid reader choosing a book depends mostly on preferences about genre, author, length, etc. But for many graphic designers the books we choose to read depend largely on the cover design. So it should come as no surprise to you that you have probably read a book with a cover designed by CHIP KIDD. At least one of his, approximately, 800 cover designs.

His work has graced the covers of books written by every best-selling author (at least in the US) from Michael Crichton's LOST WORLD to David Sedaris' NAKED, one of my all time favorite books. But there is no need to list all of his covers.

A writer himself, he recently published THE CHEESE MONKEYS: A NOVEL IN TWO SEMESTERS, a fiction novel that relates to graphic design (I haven't read it, but it's the next one on my list). He has published various books about BATMAN, a subject with which he has a strong, and strange, FASCINATION.

His work has been published in every major publication, and has also contributed with design magazines, providing insightful, and always amusing, writing and commentary.

Truly, an influential designer.

POSTED BY **ARMIN** on 09.25.2002 | COMMENTS [9]

TIMELESS

So I'm sitting here with my coffee and I'm feeling nostalgic.

Explanations, critiques or opinions are not necessary for RAÚL RAÑA.

POSTED BY **ARMIN** on 09.25.2002 | COMMENTS [9]

SIGN UP FOR TYPEFACE TAG

From the people at Type Club:

Each player will have 24 hours to contribute to an original typeface, creating three new characters inspired by previous letters. Over many turns where the most desirable traits are emphasized players should evolve a mutually agreeable alphabet. When the typeface is complete, it will be compiled and distributed to all. Submit name and email for play at TYPE CLUB.

*At this moment I have the file for the following as hours (give or take, depending on when you read this). I'm thinking mustaches as far as the eye can see :( ]

POSTED BY **ARMIN** on 09.23.2002 | COMMENTS [9]

Design: Think, Make, Do.
a graduate studies "do-tank"
Indiana University
Herron School of Art & Design

Want to Advertise on UnderConsideration?
E-Mail Us

Recommended Reading ▸ SEE ALL

Random Selections From our Selection
(To See All, Click)

The Word It Book: Speak Up presents a gallery of interpreted words

Off-Kilter

design: The Anatomy of Design

Join our Mailing List

Name (Required)

E-mail (Required)

City (Optional)

▸ sign me up
▸ unsubscribe

Also by UnderConsideration

BRAND NEW

Covering the most relevant and creative on and offline the first portal to the design community — and said community is openly invited and encouraged to aid their hard earned flow.

+DE
the design encyclopedia

Describing, tracking and explaining culture, commerce, politics, media, scams, brands — everything possible, really — through design.

Qs / Vol. 11 / November 5 - November 11

The top 15 out of a 37-quip week.

By Armin on Nov.12.2007 ▸ Link ▸ Comments [3]

"What is a Typeface?" Alex

[Answer: This is the correct way of calling a Font]

This past Wednesday, November 7th, 2007, the show *Jeopardy* presented its 5,328th show, the quarterfinal of the Tournament of Champions. In the *Double Jeopardy!* Round, the three contestants were faced with the following category:

Continue reading this entry

By Armin on Nov.09.2007 ▸ Link ▸ Comments [20]

Jury Duty

Over the last couple of weeks I have slowly passed the 2007 edition of Print's *Regional Design Annual* — one of the heftiest magazine annuals around. Unlike other years, browsing this annual was a pleasure. The images were big, the captions were easy to match with the numbers, and the 1,026 entries felt integrated in a way that no other Regional had before, in their typically headache-inducing collection of postage-sized thumbnails and finger-bending, hand-cramping weight. (I skimmed it every year, no matter.) But it was through this newfound clarity and accessibility — enabling me to spend more time looking at and considering the winning entries and passing judgment of my own — that a long brewing set of concerns about this collection in particular and a larger question about design judging in general bubbled to the top of my to-poke list.

Continue reading this entry

By Armin on Nov.07.2007 ▸ Link ▸ Comments [35]

Qs / Vols. 10 - 11 / October 29 - November 4

The top 15 out of a 39-quip week.

By Armin on Nov.05.2007 ▸ Link ▸ Comments [4]

Tennis, Anyone?

Bonnie and Clyde. Scarlett and Rhett. Bogie and Bacall. Butch and Sundance. Thelma and Louise. All great friends or great lovers or great adversaries. Every once in a while, they are all three. But in some way or another, these celebrated duos have come to embody what it means to be great partners. On Friday, November 2nd at 2:00 PM Central time, you can add Bantjes and Vit to the list. Or more accurately put, Bantjes vs. Vit.

By debbe millman on Oct.31.2007 ▸ Link ▸ Comments [14]

The Mommy Track: Six Months In

It was six months ago that I announced to the world I was knocked up and unemployed. Now, as I did then, I find myself in a totally different situation than the one I had planned so carefully — one that, though flexible in theory, did not stretch as far as I hoped. The worst part of it all? I was not as flexible as I needed to be.

Continue reading this entry

By bryony on Oct.25.2007 ▸ Link ▸ Comments [14]

Small Design Ephemera: The Endeavor

As Bryony and I settle UnderConsideration as a working day-to-day business in its official digs, we have been moving things around, rearranging this that and the other, and, inevitably, getting rid of stuff we don't need — like my collection of 32 (and growing) empty tins of peppermint Altoids (verdict: it lives!). There is one pile of belongings that has survived this recurring cleansing process for more than eight years, and three major moves, despite my acknowledgment of its place in the Stuff We Don't Need category: My Design Stuff.

Continue reading this entry

By Armin on Oct.24.2007 ▸ Link ▸ Comments [11]

By: Jeff Barlow

▸ Next
▸ Look
▸ Collaborate

Search

Enter keywords

▸ go find it!

Archives

By Month

By Category

The design was still inconspicuous, though, and lacking any real statement. In mid-2007, with three blogs, one wiki, and a design firm all grouped beneath the umbrella of UnderConsideration, we *needed* a much nicer design for that section. It is a typographic-driven website, based on aesthetics, a fact which gives us joy. The UnderConsideration section is now a few pages deep, and tells our story rather nicely. By displaying live feeds of our sites, it remains consistently updated.

RIGHT:

UnderConsideration, 2002.

UnderConsideration, 2006.

UnderConsideration, 2007.

THE ESSENTIAL PRINCIPLES OF GRAPHIC DESIGN

UNDER CONSIDERATION LLC

FORMED 2007
ESTABLISHED 2001

WHAT THIS IS

A growing network and enterprise dedicated to the progress of the graphic design profession and its practitioners, students and enthusiasts. At times intangible, its purpose is to question, push, analyze and agitate graphic design and those involved in the profession. *More about UnderConsideration...*

THINGS TO DO AROUND HERE

1 / Find out about the newly minted Department of Design
2 / You could learn about the hard-working founders
3 / Peruse a list of current contributors
4 / Get an idea of what our ADVx3 advertising is all about
5 / Or just enjoy the lively sites that make up this corner of the internet by scrolling down, reading and clicking where necessary

THE UNDERCONSIDERATION ONLINE NETWORK / INFO - RECENT ACTIVITY

Speak Up

underconsideration.com/speak-up
Discussing, and looking for, what is relevant in, and the relevance of, graphic design.
More about Speak Up...

RECENT ACTIVITY / RSS

"What is a Typeface?" Alex
Posted on Nov.9.2007 by Armin

Jury Duty
Posted on Nov.7.2007 by Armin

Qs / Vols. 10 - 11 / October 29 - November 4
Posted on Nov.5.2007 by Armin

Tennis, Anyone?
Posted on Oct.31.2007 by debbie millman

Landmark Web Sites, Where Art Thou?
Posted on Oct.30.2007 by Armin

BRAND NEW

underconsideration.com/brandnew
Displaying opinions, and focusing solely on corporate and brand identity work.
More about Brand New...

RECENT ACTIVITY / RSS

A Swing and a Miss
On Nov.8.2007 By JonSel

I Ahearts; Wolff Olins
On Nov.7.2007 By Armin

Enterprise gets Unionized
On Nov.6.2007 By JonSel

Applebee's Gets A Spokesapple
On Nov.5.2007 By John Feldhouse

Shriners Face Forward
On Nov.3.2007 By Brand New

QUIPSOLOGIES

underconsideration.com/quipsologies
Corralling the most relevant and creative on- and off-line bits that pertain to the design community.
More about Quipsologies...

RECENT ACTIVITY / RSS AUTHORS, COMMUNITY

Quipsologies : From the Authors

Vol. 11 | No. 43
The brand quilt. Literally.

Vol. 11 | No. 42
Now Then, an online exhibit at MoCCA of artists and [...]

Vol. 11 | No. 41
Information Graphics, the Rap edition. Some language NSFW. [Via BuzzFeed]

Vol. 11 | No. 40
Free Magento! [See No. 15 below]

Vol. 11 | No. 39
"Gertel's will likely be survived by a condominium. Luxury, and [...]

Quipsologies : From the Community

Vol. 11 | No. 19
A 4 minute short on Paul Rand. Courtesy of [...]

Vol. 11 | No. 18
Waterlollies. Adam Phillips continues to push the Flash medium. [...]

Vol. 11 | No. 17
Design is a process, not a product! Amen to that [...]

Vol. 11 | No. 16
The IFC Blog takes a look at some recent tv [...]

Vol. 11 | No. 15
Postcards from our awesome future where you can work out [...]

the design encyclopedia

thedesignencyclopedia.org
Describing, tracking and explaining culture, commerce, politics, media, sports and brands through design.
More about TDE...

RECENT ACTIVITY / RSS

/society_for_news_design
Last updated on Oct.31.2007

/fred_smeijers
Last updated on Oct.21.2007

/ourtype
Last updated on Oct.21.2007

/jennifer_sterling
Last updated on Sep.21.2007

/tibor_kalman
Last updated on Sep.21.2007

NEWS

October 2007

UC.DOD Opens
UnderConsideration now operates its Department of Design to serve clients and their myriad needs, as well as to develop its own design requirements.

July 2007

DESIGN LIFE NOW
NATIONAL DESIGN TRIENNIAL 2006

Triennial's Last Days
Last chance, before another three years have to go by. Stop by the Cooper-Hewitt before July 29 to catch the Triennial and spot Speak Up.

UCDA Conference
Armin will be speaking at the 2007 UCDA Design Conference in Toronto, Canada.

May 2007

3 x 3 = Good Advertising
With four web sites running on all internet cylinders through UnderConsideration, we have established an exclusive advertising program, dubbed 3 x 3, that guarantees 33% of all page impressions. Interested? Intrigued? Inquire.

April 2007

The Word It Book
After almost a year of designing and producing, *The Word It Book: Speak Up presents a gallery of integrated words* published by HOW Books is now shipping. And, because we like you so much, we have put together a behind-the-scenes look of some of our favorite photos.

February 2007

Art Directors Club Judging
Bryony served on the jury for the Art Directors Club 96th Annual Awards in the Graphic Design category.

Type Directors Club Judging
Armin served on the jury for the Type Directors Club TDC53 competition.

January 2007

Complete News Archive...

A FEW MORE DETAILS

UnderConsideration LLC
583 17th Street
First Floor
Brooklyn, NY 11219
p. (718) 499-4962
f. (718) 228-0720
e. info@underconsideration.com

Quick (Outbound) Links
Department of Design
Speak Up
Brand New
Quipsologies
The Design Encyclopedia

Quick (Inbound) Links
Founders
Contributors
About

Good Code
With exceptions found in the feeds, UnderConsideration is W3C compliant and a valid XHTML 1.0 Transitional.

CHIRP!

PROJECT

CBS Rebrand

DESIGNER

Jakob Trollbäck, Trollbäck & Associates

CLIENT

CBS

I try to get people to use their brains. Computers are not very helpful—it is too tempting to create visuals before the arrival of an actual idea. I try to find the spirit of a project, to grasp at the ungraspable details that will make the piece work. The question is: what can we do to make this special and emotionally relevant to people?

Design is just like any other expressive skill. You must master the discipline to be able to use it, and you must have something important to say. If you mastered the French language, would you use it to merely rattle off nice-sounding words? You want to have message and context. Without these, it's just baby talk. Design's main problem is that it can look cool without saying anything. People are tempted to put shapes together, meld colors and type, just for the hell of it. *Je voulez voudrais s'il vous plait un chavalle du auto dans la sur de la cote, cheri.* Yes, exactly.

RIGHT:
The original identity for the CBS television network.

campaign consisted of a montage of great moments compiled from the network's programs. This was accompanied by bold interstitials and a design tweak.

The goal was to essentially give the network a new face, while drawing a parallel between the CBS brand and its programming. Designers highlighted the popularity of the programming by imbuing their creative structure with pride and enthusiasm, the very essence of which were reflected by the network itself. They placed the CBS "eye" logo in a trademark position on show titles, days of the week, and descriptive words—a direct approach which respected the value of the logo. In addition to this, the designers placed the words "We are" in front of the CBS eye, similarly positioning it for popular programs and genres. The result was a flexible campaign that seamlessly morphed into strong slogans such as, "We are Survivor," and "We are Comedy," which naturally led to "We are CBS."

"Every moment... Every hour... Every day... Every feeling... We are excitement... America's most watched network."

SURVIVOR: EXILE ISLAND®   THURSDAY

EVERY MOMENT

OUR

EVERY DAY

EVERY FEELING

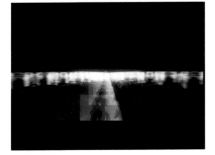

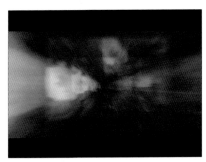

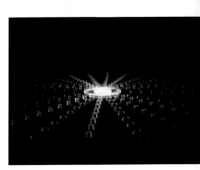

WE ARE

AMERICA'S MOST WATCHED NETWORK

ABOVE:
Navigation endpages for CBS.

AMERICA'S MOST
WATCHED NETWORK

VIVOR

R NEXT

CBS.com

ACTION

WE ARE CBS

PROJECT

Video Music Brasil

DESIGNER

Fernando Leal

CLIENT

MTV Brasil

I have an illustrative style, based on collage, so when I begin a project, I study collections of imagery, textures, and fonts for inspiration. I have sketchbooks for drawing, computers for fonts, and layouts for textures and images. Some designers preach that you must begin with a sketchbook and avoid the computer at all costs until it becomes a necessary tool. I find this argument irrelevant, especially since I work with collage, which can be manipulated on the screen.

Usually, I create A3 (Tabloid) documents in Photoshop and produce layers and layers using texture, type, and images. It's crucial not to concern yourself with the final product at this point. Once the imagery and ideas surface—and they will—then you can start thinking about fitting everything into a specific format and medium. You have to trust yourself and trust your creativity; allow the human to work before the machine takes over.

If I'm working on a CD cover, or a bit of TV animation—if the space is more vertical and horizontal—I will have to create an illustration. This allows the format to reside in the back of my head without impeding any ideas that would like to shoot to the forefront. An A3 document is spacious enough to play around with.

ABOVE:
Type explorations.

RIGHT:
Logo explorations.

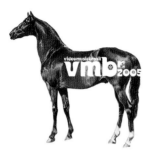

MTV Brasil

I was a full-time hire with MTV Brasil when I designed the logos
for the VMB (Video Music Brasil) awards in 2005. Since it was a
huge and detailed endeavor, every department in the company was
involved. When I designed the promos and titles for other shows on
MTV, the promo department manager had final approval; the VMB
required several versions of the show's logo, created by multiple
directors, and was overseen by the entire board of directors.

The chosen theme that year was "kitsch." I began with the type,
mixing fonts and composing the integration of the two distinct
company logos, MTV and VMB. I still had to evoke the "kitsch"
theme, which is why I applied the type and graphics to the old
Victorian imagery. Once my logo was approved, my workmates in
the promo department suggested I add something subversive to the
imagery. You can see that I took their advice—the horse losing its
head, the ice cream struck by the axe, and so on.

It is essential to experiment with ideas that go beyond the pale.
Sometimes, by creating a logo that is contrary to its actual intention,
or by skewing a message and introducing the dying art of irony, a
designer can provoke a stronger and more interesting reaction from
the viewer. The methods and inspirations one uses in the creation
of logos vary from case to case. As design is such a broad discipline,
it's important to remain flexible, and to never turn away from a
project that challenges you. Sometimes a client can brief you to
death, but this shouldn't be a reason to turn down a commission.
If you're confident with your style, then you don't have to concern
yourself with selling out, because the work that pours forth will
naturally be outside the spectrum and, therefore, distinctive.

TOP LEFT:
Early versions of the VMB logo
for MTV Brasil.

BOTTOM LEFT
Final logos.

SOUND BITES

On Starting a Project

Alberto Rigau: I begin with text. I make lists of terminology related to the project. Let's say I was working on the signage for a construction project: I'd scribble the words "concrete tilt-up, bauxite, reinforced steel." It's a written map of communications, synonyms and antonyms, and of common denominators. When I have enough of a mess in my sketchbook, I sort everything out, and shortly afterward, conceptualization and drawing can begin. My designs are never final in my sketchbook. Once in the computer, they morph and adapt to their digital environment. Identity systems and special projects (like exhibits or 3-D) always go through a hand-worked phase. Invitations and newsletters require a different model altogether. In the end, every project calls for a distinct process.

Fabian Monheim: I usually begin a project by tidying the scene of any old, unrelated bits of work. I follow this with extensive and intensive research, exploring topics in order to find relevant visuals. Once I'm onto something interesting, I st ep back for a few days and allow the ideas and visuals to simmer in my head. Soon enough, the imagery begins to percolate. It doesn't necessarily have to occur during work hours. It could happen on a bus or a tram. And once I have two to three feasible ideas, I start to put pencil to paper.

Josh Chen: No matter how the industry changes, along with the inherent technology, intelligent, authentic ideas will always be the prime communicant. Designers are perpetually searching for the perfect execution of an idea. Sometimes, the harder they look, the less likely they are to find it.

This is because the unexpected moments are what truly count, the off-the-cuff happenings, the flying in the face of convention that inspires great art and makes for the great memories of life. Those who have the skills and the talent for this communicative creativity will always be needed. Good ideas never go the way of the Old West; they do not fade into the sunset. In the ultimate design showdown, once the tower clock strikes in the hush of noonfall, the Idea will outdraw Technology without breaking a sweat, leaving it panting in the dust every single time.

Simon Waterfall: At Poke we do a lot of homework. The project success for us lies in the first five percent and the last five percent. The first five percent is research, trendspotting, technical scoping, and the client meeting. The last five percent is time left for polishing and really urging the beauty out of the design. The middle 90 percent is a mix of many processes, as we work collaboratively with many agencies and individuals, and very little is similar.

Deborah Adler: Assignments and ideas reside in my head for a long while before I begin working. I problem-solve and strategize before the pencil even scratches paper. I spend a great length of time researching and listening. Once I hear the necessary click, I bring out the sketchpad or hop onto the computer and make it all happen. I usually work until I begin to lose interest, and that's when I slink off to allow the hot idea to cool down a bit before I add the necessary refinements. Eventually, I end up with two or three solutions worth presenting.

Marian Bantjes: I am first and foremost a visual designer. My work may often contain conceptual elements, but this is not where I begin. Usually, I have a fairly immediate vision of what I want the piece to be like. The final piece may not correspond to my original visualization, but this is part of the birth pangs of the process. I do not create exploratory sketches; I do not dabble; I know exactly what I want. The primary challenge involves the struggle of making the imaginary into something concrete. The beginning is often very simple for me. I sketch with a pencil, and, depending on what I scan into the computer, Photoshop it. Soon after it's printed, I'll redraw it by hand until it's exactly how I want it. If the final sketch is to be in vector art, I scan it and trace it by hand in Illustrator—I never use live trace or any other auto-tracing software. Finally, I make very careful adjustments, so that all the curves are perfect. The end result is usually very close to the sketch, only far cleaner, and sometimes more detailed.

Brian Rea: I always begin work by taking copious notes, making simple connections between things, and these notes usually develop into quick drawings that trigger visual ideas. Sometimes, this becomes the final idea, or in some cases the final product, but on other occasions it leads me to consider methods of problem-solving I hadn't even considered before. I often have multiple solutions to a project, and I prefer exhausting all angles before I settle on one. Restraint is a really great tool, and far too often overlooked. Whether I'm working on an illustration, book jacket, or design mural doesn't matter—the process is always the same.

Doyald Young: I start with rough sketches. Then I do more refined drawings and then I create a digitized font, and then I do the required testing.

Lucienne Roberts: I begin by reading the copy.

First Jobs

Andrea Deszö: My very first design was for a series of Hungarian books catering to middle-school children. I won the project in 1996, when I was fresh out of graduate school and desperately searching for work. The Hungarian Design Center was holding an invitational competition, to which they had invited one famous designer, one in mid-career, and a virtual unknown who— as it turned out—would be me. Anyone who submitted was to be paid a fee, which, at the time, I considered a small fortune so I went to work immediately. Now, I had no expectations beyond the fee, but my American boyfriend and future husband, Adam, motivated me with all these underdog stories and pushed me to fight. His confidence and idealism were a revelation, considering that I had come from a traditional, authoritarian culture. Growing up in Transylvania, Romania, you didn't hear too many *Rocky*-like stories, where the underdog always succeeds. So it was Adam's enthusiasm that instilled in me the confidence I needed to secure the project.

Patrick Thomas: I won my first commission in 1986, when I was studying at Saint Martin's School of Art [now Central Saint Martins College], in London. It was a small spot illustration for the wine section of the Sunday color supplement of the London-based *Observer* newspaper.

Luba Lukova: Shortly after I graduated from the National Arts Academy (in Sofia, Bulgaria), I created a silk-screened poster for a production based on Federico Garcia Lorca's poetry, entitled *There is no Death for the Songs.* The imagery was directly inspired by Lorca's poetry, whose recurring themes are love, death, and music. This is why the guitar bleeds like a human being—struck by the pain of music and love, and run through with daggers. What I found particularly interesting was the political meaning people derived from the work when they saw it plastered on the walls, which was not what I had intended. A friend in those days called it "culture being stabbed in the back," and I remember liking that interpretation. After all, this was in 1986, when Bulgaria was still under communist rule.

Bennett Peji: I landed my first corporate identity projects nearly 20 years ago—beating several established design firms—while I was still a senior in college. The projects were for a long-distance telephone company and a regional bank respectively, and they eventually turned into full accounts. I did it all—their logos, business stationery, annual reports, vehicle graphics, uniforms, and billboards—and these clients referred me to dozens of others. Before I knew it, I was in business.

David Gibson: I distinctly remember the first cold calls I ever made, shortly after starting my firm, Two Twelve Associates, in 1980: "Hello. My name is David Gibson, and I'm a recent graduate of Yale's graphic design program. I recently started a design firm called Two Twelve Associates, and we're interested in working with cultural institutions." By that leap of trembling faith, we won several loyal clients, including the International Center for Photography and the Municipal Art Society. I'll never forget those first calls and the massive assault of nerves— my excitement at just having started my own

design firm, my passion for the craft, and my uncertainty about the entire enterprise. And I will never forget the clients who consented to hear my amateurish pitch and took a chance on a fledgling company 28 years ago.

Matteo Bologna: I'm a self-taught designer. I learned my skills in Italy, literally copying from the Type Directors Club annuals. The first time I submitted my work to a design competition, it was selected for the twentieth Club annual. I'd created an identity for Balthazar's restaurant, and any hopes I'd had of being selected were quite low. To my surprise, not only had my work been selected, but it was also the Judge's Choice.

Ruedi Baur: In 1978, there was a poster contest for the International Child of the Year, so I submitted Unser Jahr/Notre Année (Our Year), which I completed with Lars Müller. We sought to transcend the official nature of the theme, to produce something that the public could approach with some ease. Hence the slogan, "Our Year," in child's handwriting.

Hillman Curtis: In 1998, I quit Macromedia to start my own company. I was renting a desk at the old Razorfish office on Broome Street when I received a call from a gentleman who was running an outfit called SonicNet Radio. This was one of the first online radio stations, and Intel was placing ads on site. This gentleman introduced me to his advertising agency in Salt Lake City, Utah. They were handling the Intel account, and I became the designer of little flash ads, earning $500 per ad.

Khoi Vinh: When I left art school with my painting and illustration portfolio in tow, I knew that I wanted to be a graphic designer. The mechanics of the field appealed to me immensely: the typography, the juxtaposition of word and image, the transmission of ideas. Graphic design is all about context, and this is a concept that I find enthralling. I took a job with a small advertising agency in the Washington DC area that focused primarily on commercial and residential real estate. I was so happy to be in the field that I didn't care what I was designing, so long as I had the opportunity to practice the craft. My coworkers and I spent an exorbitant amount of time developing pitch work—billboards, advertisements, T-shirts, and all kinds of collateral. All this was centered on a cartoon kangaroo that I'd drawn. We had a great time, though in the end they decided not to use the kangaroo.

Fernando Leal: My first major project was in 2000. I was working as a graphic designer with Lobo, a well-known firm at the time for their experimentation in different medias. Lobo was under corporate pressure to release a comedy-based website which targeted teenage boys, and I was hired as the art director for the site, which surprised me, because I had little professional experience in this area. It was a difficult, high-pressure job, and we churned out crude toilet humor in a quick and unsophisticated manner. It was fantastic when we got involved in designing the layouts and logos, but this wasn't enough to surpass the basic fact that I had to produce garbage that didn't interest me.

Christoph Niemann: My first New York job was an illustration for *Rolling Stone*. I was Paul Davis's intern, and he introduced me to Fred Woodward at an Art Directors Club event. I got a call from Fred two days before I was due back in Germany for an assignment. I cursed myself for taking on the job with so little time, but when Fred Woodward calls you, you don't say no. I was sure that if I screwed this one up I would never work in the city again. I was so anxious, I didn't sleep until the job was finished. When I returned to Germany, I kept running to the international newsstand in Stuttgart to look for the issue, and I couldn't believe it when I actually found it.

Per Mollerup: The first project we ever won was a corporate identity job for the technological service organization Jysk Teknologisk Institut (The Jutland Institute of Technology). A shortening of the name to Jysk Teknologisk and a new logo were central elements in our solution. The new logo featured a capital J with cogs. The cogs were a welcome reference to the previous logo that featured two gear wheels.

Etienne Mineur: The first project I won was for Canal, a television channel in France, over 15 years ago. I was hired to create an interactive CD-ROM about music. Back then, everything was new (and hardly anyone knew about interactive design), and we had a lot of opportunity since no one knew what they were doing in this new medium! Fifteen years later, I'm still working with them, though, thankfully, we all know a lot more about what we're doing.

Simon Waterfall: The first job I ever won was when I was 16. Together with a partner, I had a computer games company called Silicon Genetics. We designed computer games for Commodore 64s and Amigas. Luckily, they have all been destroyed, but in essence, I still have the same role now as I did 20 years ago. I just have a few more qualifications and a lot more facial hair.

Doyald Young: A logo for an upscale dress shop in Pasadena named Helen Smith.

Lucienne Roberts: Setting type by hand and using 19th Century Albion Presses.

On Making Mistakes

Peter Buchanan Smith: My biggest mistakes can always be attributed to my fears. Unless they are catastrophic, mistakes by nature are fleeting. They are eventually set right and recover quite nicely through the passage of time. I look back on my mistakes with a certain amount of adoration, for they've made me who I am. Still, the hardest mistake to bounce back from is the one that hurts someone else. Doing or saying something to deflate an individual's confidence is the worst mistake that I could think of.

Branko Lucic: When I was 19 I was hired to create a series of gigantic billboards for the concert venue SKC, in Belgrade, Serbia. It was impossible to have them printed, so I was forced to paint them all by hand as large murals.

Jiae Kim: When we make mistakes, it's usually because we didn't trust our instincts, and we didn't take the time to really work out the design.

Bryony Gomez Palacio: My mistakes usually stem from a lack of sleep. This leads to distraction, a foregoing of details that could land me in the cannibal soup: typos, a missed change, missing supporting files, writing incomplete specs, and a host of other minor disasters. Individually, the mistakes are miniscule, but when they tend to accumulate in one week, or in one particular project, I sink deeper and faster into the sludge. For me, the best thing to do is to shut down the computer, take a long nap, and restart with a gigantic cup of coffee and an updated calendar, so that I can re-attack with renewed vigor.

Simon Waterfall: The biggest mistake I have ever made I hope will be tomorrow.

Khoi Vinh: I've made the mistake, several times, of thinking that I could do great design for clients and projects in which I didn't believe. I've worked in idioms that weren't comfortable for me, but which I initially thought were "easy." Ultimately, the work I did for those was less than my best. A truly great designer can design almost anything, it's true, but no designer can do truly great work unless they truly have a passion for the challenge at hand.

Marian Bantjes: When I first started out in my own design studio, I made a million mistakes. I didn't deal properly with clients, printers, staff, and, worst of all, my business partner. Most of my mistakes stemmed from the concept of working for money. I earn an income now, but I still can't afford to be picky. To satisfy something deep within me, I really need to be interested in a project, to have a glimpse of some future potential beyond the client's expectations. What I require most of all is a work of absolute complexity, so that I can experience the joy of problem-solving.

Lucienne Roberts: I always try to bring humility to my work and acknowledge that ours is a job that involves others. I believe that "good" work is as much the result of empathy between client and designer as the designer's talent or expertise. But, as someone who truly believes that design can make the world a better place, I should be telling people this more often and with greater force.

On Lessons Learned

Richard Colbourne: Fifteen years ago, in London, I designed an annual report for a British McDonald's. I remember being very nervous as I presented the final photography to the client, because I had interpreted the brief in a radical way and spent the entire budget doing it. I always use my intuition when I interpret a brief creatively. Since I immerse myself in the relevant information, my intuition behaves more like the truth: understanding and interpreting is ultimately the same thing. To my relief, McDonald's loved the photos, and I learned an important lesson: if you aren't nervous enough in a presentation, then you haven't pushed the envelope.

John Gall: Early on in my career, I was given a very small budget with instructions to hire an illustrator. The illustrator I wanted to work with wanted a particular fee for a full-color illustration, and considerably less for a black-and-white illustration. My brilliant idea was to purchase the black-and-white illustration at the cheaper price and color it myself. I couldn't have been more wrong. I would have been better off taking the entire budget and blowing it at a racetrack.

Matteo Bologna: My first paying job was for a neighborhood grocer who had heard that I was an art student. He asked me to make a couple of sales items for his shop window. In a span of two weeks, using a ruling pen, gouache, and French curves, I looked to reauthenticate the vernacular of the grocery-store sale sign. I was paid $10 for my aesthetics. Lesson learned: take a business class and leave the "vernacular" to the professionals, who never refer to "vernacular" in the first place.

Alberto Rigau: I once took for granted information given to me by a client, concerning a project's audience, and, because I was in a rush, based my designs on what I'd been told. Once the piece came out and I recognized its context, I saw that I had designed it all wrong. Ever since then, I've always insisted upon conducting my own research.

Marian Bantjes: I'm often asked to create pieces that bear close relation to my past work, and I never hesitate to reject projects that outright reflect what has been done previously. As far as I'm concerned, it's up to me to take the risk, and this in turn will show the client how to leap. My very best work comes from the open brief, and I am sympathetic to the fact that such a brief is a very scary place for a client to be, so I applaud their bravery when they agree to move forward.

Brian Rea: When I was in the third grade, I submitted a coloring-contest entry to the local drug store. First prize was an awesome bike with yellow mag wheels. I came in second and was crushed. The following year I tried again, adding colors that to my mind had never even existed, going so far as to mount the end result on navy-blue construction paper. I won the bike that year and a lesson was learned: a passionate presentation counts.

Words of Wisdom

Fabian Monheim: In graphic design, it is essential to commit oneself to work that is very personal, for this creates a proving ground which provides ample space to test one's limits and endurance. Most importantly, these forays into the personal feed the commercial work. Graphic design is not about offering a service, and it is most certainly not about personal expression. There is a great divide between commercial and personal projects.

Simon Waterfall: Work with people who are much more talented than you are. If you are learning all the time you will stay engaged and you will be able to keep up. A designer should never cruise with the current, otherwise they will become rudderless and restless, which we know is not good for creativity. The currency of creativity is failure. It means you're trying. Never, never design to win awards, be best in class, or go for the easy points. You'll hate your work.

Fernando Leal: There have been certain points in my career when I've had to stop and think things out. It's hard to remain focused when you're set adrift by the double lures of money and exposure. If you don't set goals concerning the kind of design you want to create—historical, critical, subversive—then who you want to become will not be reflected by the contents of your portfolio. You will become a machine controlled by the dull demands of your career. It is essential to experiment with all media, styles, and clients. And it is equally important to learn how to say "no."

Alberto Rigau: Graphic design is much more than form-making. Our work gives people the tools to create meaningful experiences in their everyday lives. We are responsible for the visual shaping of the culture; in short, we are the gatekeepers.

Erik Spiekermann: Without knowledge, you cannot afford an attitude, and without an attitude, you cannot be credible and reach people. And without people, this can become a very lonely business.

Peter Buchanan-Smith: The biggest thing I've learned is that I must constantly design with the notion in the forefront of my mind that nothing is impossible, and almost everything is impossible.

Per Mollerup: The most important thing for graphic design is an expanded application of a saying by the Austrian philosopher Ludwig Wittgenstein: "Whatever can be said, can be said clearly."

Contributors

ALBERTO RIGAU
blog.estudiointerlinea.com

ANDREA DESZÖ
a.parsons.edu/~andi

ANDY JOHNSON
www.uniteddsn.com

ANTENNA DESIGN
www.antennadesign.com

ARMIT VIT
www.underconsideration.com

BARBARA DeWILDE
www.dewildesign.com

BENNETT PEJI
www.pejidesign.com

BILL CAHAN
www.cahanassociates.com

BRANKO LUCIC
www.nonobject.com

BRIAN REA
www.brian-rea.com

BRYONY GOMEZ-PALACIO
www.underconsideration.com

CARINE ABRAHAM
www.abraka.com

CHERYL SWANSON
www.toniq.com

CHRIS BOLTON
www.chrisbolton.org

CHRISTOPH NIEMANN
www.christophniemann.com

CONNIE BIRDSALL
www.lippincott.com

DAVID GIBSON
www.twotwelve.com

DEBORAH ADLER
www.miltonglaser.com

DOYALD YOUNG
www.doyaldyoung.com

ED FELLA
www.edfella.com

ERIK SPIEKERMANN
www.spiekermannpartners.com

ETIENNE MINEUR
www.incandescence.com

FABIAN MONHEIM
www.flyproduction.jp

FERNANDO LEAL
www.fleal.com

GAEL TOWEY
www.marthastewart.com

HILLMAN CURTIS
www.hillmancurtis.com

JAKOB TROLLBÄCK
www.trollback.com

JIAE KIM
www.thememagazine.com

JOHN FOSTER
www.fuszion.com

JOHN FULBROOK
www.collins1.com

JOHN GALL
www.randomhouse.com

JONATHAN HOEFLER
www.typography.com

JOSH CHEN
www.chendesign.com

KATY BRIGHTON
www.sterlingbrands.com

KHOI VINH
www.subtraction.com

LAWRENCE HAGGERTY
www.uniteddsn.com

LISA ROUSSEAU
www.pepperidgefarm.com

LUCIENNE ROBERTS
sans@dircon.co.uk

LUBA LUKOVA
www.lukova.net

MARIAN BANTJES
www.bantjes.com

MARK KINGSLEY
www.greenbergkingsley.com

MATTEO BOLOGNA
www.muccadesign.com

MIKE BAINBRIDGE
www.sterlingbrands.com

NICHOLAS BLECHMAN
www.knickerbocker.com

PATRICK THOMAS
www.lavistadesign.com

PER MOLLERUP
www.mollerup-designlab.com

PETER BUCHANAN-SMITH
www.buchanansmith.com

RICHARD COLBOURNE
www.addison.com

RICK VALICENTI
www.3st.com

ROB WALLACE
www.wallacechurch.com

RUEDI BAUR
www.integral.ruedi-baur.com

SATORU WAKESHIMA
www.cbx.com

SIGI MOELSLIGER
www.antennadesign.com/

SIMON WATERFALL
www.pokelondon.com/

STEPHEN DOYLE
www.doylepartners.com/

VAULT49
www.vault49.com

YVES BEHAR
www.fuseproject.com

Index